A POLICEMAN ALSO DIES
AND
OTHER PLAYS

SOLOMON C. A. AWUZIE

Mwanaka Media and Publishing Pvt Ltd,
Chitungwiza Zimbabwe
*
Creativity, Wisdom and Beauty

Publisher: *Mmap*
Mwanaka Media and Publishing Pvt Ltd
24 Svosve Road, Zengeza 1
Chitungwiza Zimbabwe
mwanaka@yahoo.com
mwanaka13@gmail.com
https://www.mmapublishing.org
www.africanbookscollective.com/publishers/mwanaka-media-and-publishing
https://facebook.com/MwanakaMediaAndPublishing/

Distributed in and outside N. America by African Books Collective
orders@africanbookscollective.com
www.africanbookscollective.com

ISBN: 978-1-77921-332-7
EAN: 9781779213327

© Solomon C. A. Awuzie 2022

ii

Acknowledgement

A Policeman also Dies and Other Stories was previously Published by

Cel-Bez Publishing Co. (Nig.) Ltd.

#7 Kagha Street, Owerri, Nigeria

08035428158

E-mail: cel_bezpublishers@yahoo.com

First Published 2017

Dedication

Chukwuleta Chukwuta:

He too has seriously argued

For a Man to either die or live

And for

Late Mrs Augusta Amarachi Awuzie:

That art may thrive.

Table of Contents

Introduction

*A**Policeman also Dies* is half taken from the 1989 newspaper report of a murder case involving a policeman and two brothers. But the urge to educate the people on the need to stand and seek for redress when their rights, or the rights of their beloved ones are abused—irrespective of the persons or bodies involved—is traceable to my early youth in Lagos. Like most people, I was not brought up in a rich area; I was brought up in the peasant area of Lagos, where the people were constantly disturbed and abused by the police. To most of us who were born and bred in Amukoko, Epe, Orile, Obalende, Badia and Ajegunle, police unjustified arrests, brutalities and abuses were no news. This is because some of us had been victims of police constant *raiding* at one time or the other in the neighbourhood.

Robbers rarely invaded us, perhaps they knew their efforts would amount to nothing. We had no reason to be worried about anything—since all those living in the neighbourhood were all poor and equal. The only problem we had were the police. The police were always looking for the poor to extort. This does not mean that every policeman at this time was bad. The problem was that the majority of them saw us as criminals— though we managed to survive.

The question is: were we all criminals because we were born in Ajegunle, Amukoko, Badia, Epe, Orile and Obalende? Does it mean also that all the others who were born in Surulere, Victoria Island, Ikoyi, Festac Town, Satellite Town, Illupeju Bypass and Ikeja were good people? These questions kept ringing in my mind and it was hell trying to resolve the puzzle. Yes, there were bad people in our areas, the same way there were bad people in the other areas, but that did not make us all criminals.

It was years after leaving these areas that I found out that what we experienced in the hands of the police were not peculiar to the police but can be said to be general human problems— problems as old as life itself. One of these problems is the fact that Humans like to oppress the weak and extort money from the needy. This, as a matter of fact, can be described using the German term Schadenfreude. Schadenfreude is born when we develop what I call "obsessive self-love"—a situation where an individual loves himself more than he loves his country, the people around him and his job. We see this also exhibited in *The Haunted, The Earthworms, The Parasite* and *The Face of Love,* though differently.

Solomon Awuzie

Edo University, Iyamho

2016

A Policeman also Dies

CHARACTERS

Corporal Obi Ibe

Corporal Ayinde

Corporal Salam   police officers

Sergeant Okoro

D.P.O

Policemen

Barrister Femi }   the prosecuting counsel

Barrister Oka

Barrister Ade   }   the defence counsel

Barrister Nkeiru

Judge

Clerk

Orderly

Oluwasegun   the witnesses

Mrs Adekunle   the deceased persons'
                    mother

Olu

Yemi   }   the deceased persons

People

ACT ONE

As light comes on stage, we see people coming into the courtroom through the door that is very close to the gallery. As they come in, they are heard discussing issues relating to the day's case.

Man (1):   I want to see how the police will manoeuvre this case.

Man (11): She should forget about this case.   They always have their ways.

Enter a fat lawyer and a slim lady lawyer with files. The noise in the foyer increased. Enter another short lawyer with tribal marks and another tall lawyer. The noise becomes intense. And within a few seconds, two warders lead Ibe, Ayinde, and Salam into the courtroom.

Clerk: Court! (*Everybody in the courtroom stands up. The judge emerges from the door that is close to the bench, in his robe of black and white and a very long wig. He takes his seat and then everybody in the courtroom sits down. After a moment, theClerk stands to read out the day's case.*) Suit number HOL/27P/1989. The State versus Obi Ibe, A Ayinde, and P. Salam   (*The Clerk gives the file to the judge and sits.*)

Judge: Can we see the prosecuting counsel?

(The short lawyer with tribal marks stands up)

Barrister Femi: My lord, I'm Barrister Femi Olaolorunpo for the prosecuting counsel and with me here *(points at the nearby lawyer)* is my colleague, Barrister Oka.

Judge: *(To Barrister Oka)* Barrister Oka what?

Barrister Oka: Barrister Chima Oka, my lord.

(The judge notes it and raises his head again to the court.)

Judge: Is the defence counsel present?

Barrister Ade: Yes. My lord.

Judge: Yes!

Barrister Ade: My lord, I'm Barrister Wale Ade for the defence counsel and I'm with a colleague...

Barrister Nkeiru: My lord, my name is Barrister Nkeiru Ololo.

Judge: You said you are for the defence counsel?

Barrister Nkeiru: Yes, my lordship! *(The judge notes it)*

Judge: The prosecuting counsel may now present his case. *(Barrister Femi stands up)*

Barrister Femi: *(clears his throat)* My lord, the matter before us involves the murder of two innocent sons of a widow by these policemen. My lord, I have always known that one of the duties of the police is to save and protect the lives of

11

Nigerians and not to join robbers and criminals in killing them...

Judge: Okay (*pauses and glances at the file.*) Let's hear from the defence counsel. (*Barrister Ade stands up.*)

Barrister Ade: My lord, sometimes in situations of unrest, people lose their lives and that was what happened to the two sons of the widow, Mrs Adekunle. My client did not intentionally fired at them. It was in the process of scaring the group of rioters away that bullets accidentally discharged from the gun and killed the boys...

Judge: The accused may now be made to swear to oath. (*The Clerk moves close to Corporals Ibe, Ayinde and Salam in the accused box.*)

Clerk: Are you a Christian or a Muslim?

Obi Ibe: (*Amidst shaking lips.*) I ... I'm a Christian. (*The Clerk puts aside the Qu'ran and hands him the Holy Bible. Ibe collects it with a shivering hand.*)

Clerk: Repeat after me! (*notices that Ibe is holding the Holy Bible upside down.*) Please, re-position the Holy Bible.

Obi Ibe: (*repeats*) Please, re-position the Holy Bible. (*The Clerk becomes furious. He snatches the Holy Bible from him and re-positions it into his hand.*)

Clerk: Okay, repeat after me. (*Obi Ibe nods his head.*) In the name of Almighty God...

Obi Ibe: In the name of Almighty God ...

Clerk: …I swear that all what I'm going to say in this court …

Obi Ibe: …I swear that all what I'm going to say in this court …

Clerk: …shall be the truth.

Obi Ibe: …shall be the truth.

Clerk: Nothing but the truth.

Obi Ibe: Nothing but the truth.

Clerk: So help me God.

Obi Ibe: So help me God.

Clerk: Amen.

Obi Ibe: Amen.

Clerk: (*turns to the judge.*) My lord, the accused is on oath.

Judge: Okay!

Clerk: (*still looking into Obi Ibe's face*) Guilty or not guilty?

Obi Ibe: N... No… Not guilty, my lord!

Clerk: (*turns to the judge*) The accused pleaded not guilty, my lord.

Judge: Okay. The prosecuting counsel may now cross-examine the accused. (*Barrister Femi stands up, adjusts his robe and clears his throat*)

Barrister Femi: Why did you kill the two brothers?

Barrister Ade: (*stands up*) Objection, my lord! My learned colleague is forcing the accused to accept being guilty of the charge against him even against his will.

Judge: Objection upheld. The prosecuting counsel should remember that Mr. Obi Ibe is an accused person and ought to be treated as one.

Barrister Femi: As your lordship pleases. (*turns to Ibe*) Why did you go to the scene of the riot with a loaded and cocked rifle?

Barrister Ade: Objection, my lord! My …

Judge: Objection overruled! Corporal Ibe should answer the question.

Obi Ibe: I … I … nev … never knew the rifle was loaded.

Barrister Femi: You never knew the rifle you were carrying that day was loaded? (*pauses*) For how long have you been working as a policeman?

Obi Ibe: For fifteen years, my lord.

Barrister Femi: You've worked as a policeman for fifteen years and you still do not know when a rifle is loaded? (*Immediately, people in the gallery start laughing and talking and within few seconds the whole courtroom becomes noisy.*)

Clerk: Order! (*pauses*) I say order! (*The courtroom remains quiet again*)

14

Barrister Femi: My lord, from the few questions put forward to the accused, it is clear that the accused intentionally shot the two innocent boys.

Obi lbe: (*Holds his head suddenly*) Please, my lord; I no shoot them intentionally O!

Clerk: Order! You speak when you are asked to speak.

Judge: Mr. Obi lbe do you realize that you are in a court of law? (*Obi lbe nods*) You must be careful. (*Barrister Ade stands up and the judge signals him to talk.*) Does the defence counsel have anything to say? (*Barrister Ade stands up*)

Barrister Ade: My lord, my learned colleague felt the accused intentionally shot the two deceased boys merely because he ignorantly went to the scene of the riot with a loaded and corked rifle. How true could that be? From the information I gathered about the incident, the accused carried out two duties before the one of the riot that same day with the same rifle and did not shoot anybody. (*pauses*) Tell me, my lord, a man that carried out two of his duties on the same day with a loaded rifle and did not shoot at anybody, why should he decide to intentionally kill during his third assignment? (*He pauses and collects a piece from Barrister Nkeiru Ololo. He reads it and continues again.*) Anybody who is told the situation on ground before the accused and his other police colleagues arrived the scene, would not blame the accused. (*pauses*) My lord, I plead you permit me to ask the accused to tell the court what happened at the scene of the riot.

Judge: The accused can go on.

Barrister Ade: Mr. Obi Ibe, please, tell this honourable court what happened that day.

Obi Ibe: My lord, I just returned to the station that day with one man I arrested, when Sergeant Okoro, who dey on duty that day asked me and two of my colleagues to follow one young man wey come for our station to complain of one riot wey day happening for junction and say the police 'yellow fever' wey day there has been beaten almost to the point of death. We rushed to the junction with the young man. As we get there, the rioters come attack us. My two colleagues escaped and he come remain only me for there. They beat me so tey they come collect my gun. Before I recover from their beating, my gun shoot and somebody fell like a log of wood and the others run away. As I wan run away with my gun, one other boy come come with a very big wood and when he wan hit am for my head my gun come shoot again. (*He pauses*)

Barrister Ade: Mr Obi Ibe is that all?

Obi Ibe: No, my lord.

Barrister Ade: Then, continue.

Obi Ibe: So I come go for station and come report and them come admit me for the nearby hospital where they come treat my injuries. (*The judge notes something down.*)

Judge: Okay. Any cross-examination from the prosecuting council?

Barrister Femi: Yes, my lord.

Judge: The prosecuting counsel may now cross-examine the accused. (*Barrister Femi stands up*)

Barrister Femi: Mr. Obi Ibe, in your narration, you did not say you shot anybody. You merely said that the rifle shot them. I want you to now tell the court whether you were the person who shot the two deceased persons or the rifle shot itself.

Barrister Ade: Objection, my lord. My learned colleague is posing a confusing question to the accused.

Judge: Objectionoverruled. The accused should answer the question.

Obi Ibe: I no really know how it happened.

Barrister Femi: I mean to know whether the deceased persons were shot on the bases of either accidental discharge or in self-defence?

Obi Ibe: (*Swallows and makes up his mind.*) I no know. E be like say na accidental discharge and self-defence, my lord.

Barrister Femi: You don't confuse the court! What do you mean?

Barrister Ade: Objection, my lord. The accused has answered thequestion.

Judge: Objection upheld. The prosecuting counsel should proceed with other relevant questions.

Barrister Femi: As your lordship pleases. (*pauses*) Mr. Obi Ibe, what is the probability that the mob attacked you as soon as you and your colleagues arrived the scene?

Barrister Ade: Objection, my lord. My learned colleague should use a language that will not throw the accused off balance.

Judge: Objection upheld. The prosecuting counsel should rephrase the question.

Barrister Femi: As your lordship pleases. (*pauses*) Mr. Obi Ibe could you tell this honourable court why the rioters attacked you.

Obi Ibe: I no know, my lord .We just come and the next thing we see na the attack.

Barrister Femi: Why was it that it was you that was beaten while your other colleagues escaped?

Barrister Ade: Objection, my lord. My learned colleague is asking the accused an unimaginable question.

Judge: Objection upheld. Barrister Femi you should ask questions that will help the court to get to the root of this case.

Barrister Femi: As your lordship pleases. (*pauses*) Mr. Obi Ibe you said the rioters attacked you as soon as you got to the scene.

Obi Ibe: Yes my lord.

Barrister Femi: Butfrom the informationI got, you were not attacked when you got there.

Obi Ibe: Them attacked us, my lord!

Barrister Femi: Were your other colleagues also attacked?

Obi Ibe: Them don go when them attack me.

Barrister Femi: You mean they left you behind? But you said they escaped from the attack while you were caught and beaten.

Obi Ibe: Yes, but…. but….

Barrister Femi: My lord, I put it to the accused that he shot the two deceased persons intentionally!

Barrister Ade: Objection, my lord. My learned colleague is already condemning the accused.

Judge: Objection upheld. The prosecuting counsel should remember that the accused is still innocent of the charge until proven guilty. (*All of a sudden, a young woman starts crying and everybody in the courtroom turns towards her. She walks up to the centre stage and kneels down before the bench. And within some seconds, the courtroom becomes noisy*)

Clerk: Order!

Woman: Abeg, judge, no kill am for me. Na him be the only person wey I get.

Judge: Woman, go back to the gallery.

Woman: My lord, he get two children. If anything happens to am, I no go fit to take care of them.

Judge: Orderly! (*The policeman beside the court door quickly turns his face to the judge*)

Orderly: Yes, my lord.

Judge: Orderly, please take this woman out of the court. (*The policeman grabs the woman and drags her out of the courtroom amidst struggles and cry. After a while, the policeman returns to the court and positions himself beside the accused box. The judge adjusts his spectacle with a little push and quickly notes something down in his jotter. He later raises his face.*) The prosecuting counsel may proceed with the cross-examination.

Barrister Femi: I am done for now, my lord.

Judge: Does the defence counsel have any additional point to make?

Barrister Ade: Yes, my lord. (*pauses*) In response to what my learned colleague said, I wish to tender this picture as an exhibit. (*He stretches out the picture. The Clerk stands up and walks a little close to the bar to collect it. He returns to his seat and then stretches it out to the judge. The judge collects it, looks at it and returns it to the Clerk*)

Judge: Clerk, record it as exhibit zero one.

Clerk: Okay, my lord. (*He notes it on his register and also writes it in the back of the picture, after which he returns it to the judge.*)

Barrister Ade: You see, my lord, that picture is the picture the accused snapped immediately after the incident. That is to prove that he was actually beaten by the rioters. (*He sits down.*)

Judge: The prosecuting counsel do you have any more things to say?

Barrister Femi: Not for now, my lord.

Judge: With this, this court is adjourned to the second of August. (*He hits the gavel*)

Clerk: Court! (*Everybody in the courtroom stands up while the judge walks out through the door that is beside his bench.*)

(Snooze)

ACT TWO

As light comes on stage, we see a police station. Behind the counter are Corporal Ayinde and Corporal Salam. While Corporal Ayinde is busy writing in a notebook, Corporal Salam is seen flipping through the files that are heaped beside the counter. After a while Corporal Ayinde attracts Corporal Salam's attention.

Ayinde: I still dey wonder why he shoot them.

Salam: Well, he don kill them and there is nothing anybody can do about it. The only thing we need to do now is to protect am.

Ayinde: I know, but the way that woman dey go about the case, the thing fit result in something.

Salam: They are just wasting their time. We have already said na accidental discharge and that is final. (Enter Sergeant Okoro, with two other policemen.)

Ayinde: Oga, you don come? (*The two policemen salute Corporal Ayinde and Corporal Salam and then walk into the dressing room while Sergeant Okoro joins Corporal Ayinde and Corporal Salam behind the counter.*)

Okoro: Is that how you salute a superior officer?

Ayinde & Salam: Sorry Sir! (*They Stand erect and quickly salute him.*)

Okoro: (*ignores them.*) Has the D.P.O. *camed* to the office this morning?

22

Salam: No, Sir!

Okoro: What about Corporal Ibe?

Ayinde: He dey afternoon shift today.

Okoro: (*leaving but stops suddenly*) O! Yes, have that crazy woman *camed* here today?

Salam: You mean Mrs Adekunle?

Okoro: Yes! (*pauses, looks out of the station and returns his looks at them again.*) If she demanded that she saw Oga, don't allow her o.

Ayinde: Sir, we no dey allow her at all everyday. And every time she go wan do am by force go Oga's office.

Salam: Oga, yesterday's own was another thing. She vowed say she wouldn't go to her house. Even when we begged her, she say she would not go. Instead, she sat down there (*points*), at the passage, obstructing people's movement.

Okoro: Have her husband *camed* here too?

Ayinde: No Sir. We ask am about her husband yesterday and she say her husband don die.

Okoro: (*pauses*) Poor woman! (*pauses again*) But Corporal Salam, I have only order you to that place to make peace. Why you camed shoot? Now, you have killeded her sons.

Salam: Oga, we didn't tell am to shoot them. We were even surprised when we heard the gun shot. (*The two policemen come out from the dressing room.*)

Okoro: (*turns to them.*) Which part of the road are you going to?

Police1: Orile—Obalende road, sir. Yesterday, the policemen from the other police station told us that they made a hell lot of money on that road.

Okoro: Really?

Police 2: Oga, na so o! Drivers from those poor areas dey ever ready to give out money the moment you bark at them.

Police1: But along that Ikoyi-Victoria island road that you asked us to go yesterday nothing is there. Those fat belly, rich men and women don't give out much. What they do is to bring out their fleshy faces out from their glasses and ask you: "Hey! Officer, what is it?" And when you say: "Your pay-pass!" stretching out your hand, they quickly squeeze out their car papers onto your palm, pretending they did not understand what you meant.

Okoro: You delay them now—you told them to park by the side of the road. Corporal Tunde, is it not so?

Police 2: No be totally so, sir! Those people dey terrible. Them no dey in a hurry. And when you delay them for long, you fit put yourself for trouble.

Okoro: Is that so, Corporal Abdulahi?

Police1: Very well, sir! (*pauses*) But if it were to be on Orile—Obalende road, kai! Immediately you say "park!" so much money is squeezed into your palm.

Okoro: Okay, it was okay. You can started leaving so that you can made enough money that would be enough for all of us. (*The two policemen begin to leave while Sergeant Okoro turns to Corporal Salam and Corporal Ayinde.*)

Police1: We are going to Orile—Obalende road o.

Okoro: Of course now. It was there you will go now. (*Exit the two policemen.*)

Salam: Oga, as I was telling you, we were not the persons who tell am to shoot them. (*Sergeant Okoro is about to say something when a young man rushes into the station.*) Why are you rushing into the station like that? (*The young man gasps and looks into their faces*) Yes, how can we help you? (*The Youngman still pants*)

Young man: Officer, I dey for my house dey sleep, nayin one of my stupid neighbours come dey fight me for my room. (*pauses*) I wan arrest am.

Salam: How can somebody just come into your room to fight you? You mean, you no do anything at all – there was no previous quarrel?

Youngman: Yes! I wan arrest am. I wan deal with am—I wan deal with that stupid man.

Okoro: Young man *taked* it easy. You said the person was your neighbour? (*The Young man nods.*) Why not went home and settle your problem with him like gentlemen.

Young man: No, I wan deal with am!

Okoro: Okay, Corporal!

Salam: Sir?

Okoro: Give him sheet of paper to wrote his statement.

Salam: (*brings out a sheet of paper from under the counter and hands it over to the Youngman*) Write your statement there. (*The Youngman writes something on the paper and hands it over to Corporal Salam. Corporal Salam looks at it and files it*) Corporal Ayinde, why not you go with him while I attend to people. (*Corporal Ayinde leads the young man out of the platform*)

Okoro: Yes, Corporal, as I tolded you, all of you must insisted that it was accidental discharge, else there is problem.

Salam: That was what we wrote. Even when the woman came to the station that day that was what we told am. But what would you expect? She insisted that we show am the person who shot her sons.

Okoro: And did you showed her?

Salam: Do you want am to tear him into two? If you see the way the woman was boiling, you will need not to be told what would happen if she happened to know the person.

Okoro: Well, thank your God, it was that woman. If it was to be one of these rich people's sons you killeded, you all would have finded yourselves in a very big mess.

Salam: But we didn't tell am to do it.

Okoro: (*pauses*) I prayed you are understood.

Salam: (*looks out*) Oga, the woman is coming again o!

Okoro: Serious?

Salam: Aren't you hearing her voice?

Okoro: (*Enter Mrs Adekunle, barefooted*) Oh, she was already here.

Mrs Adekunle: (s*houting, amidst tears*) I want to see … that … stupid policeman who killed my sons! I want to see him, bring him out for me. (*hits the counter violently and quickly replaces her hands on her waist.*)

Okoro: Madam, the officer was not here. (*pauses*) He was in the hospital. Immediately after that incident, people gathereded and beat him. We pray he recovered from the attack.

Mrs Adekunle: That is not what I care. Provide him o! I want to look into his face. I want to know why my sons should die.

Salam: Madam, this is a police station; mind how you talk here. We have told you that na accidental.

Mrs Adekunle: Which accident? You have to accidentally kill me the same way you killed my sons.

Salam: Madam, go home. The D.P.O, will soon be here and might order say I throw you into the cell.

Mrs Adekunle: I want to see him. I want to know why my sons should die.

Salam: You want to sleep in the cell?

Mrs Adekunle: Let him kill me when he comes. (*Corporal Salam tries forcing her out. Enter the D.P.O.*)

D.P.O.: What is the matter here? (*Sergeant Okoro and Corporal Salam salute him.*) Can somebody tell me what is happening here? (*turns to Mrs Adekunle.*) Madam, what is the matter?

Mrs Adekunle: (*amidst tears.*) They… killed my…my Sons….

D.P.O.: Madam, look, this is a police station and we don't tolerate this rubbish here.

Mrs Adekunle: After killing my sons … oh God!

D.P.O.: Sergeant Okoro, what is this woman saying?

Okoro: Oga, it was Corporal Ibe.

D.P.O.: What happened? He killed her sons?

Okoro: No Sir? He …

Mrs Adekunle: (*cuts in*) You said no?

D.P.O.: Madam, be quiet!

Okoro: He accompanieded Corporal Salam and Corporal Ayinde to carry out arrest and along the line there was accidental discharge.

D.P.O.: (*shakes his head*) Oh! Sorry madam! (*turns to Sergeant Okoro.*) And where is Corporal Ibe?

Okoro: He … Sir … Sir (*stops and stares into the D.P.O's face.*)

D.P.O.: Madam, okay, don't worry; I will send for you later.

28

Mrs Adekunle: (*still sobbing*) I want to see him.

D.P.O.: You will see him. Just leave everything for me. (*Mrs Adekunle looks at the D.P.O. for a while and leaves, crying.*) Where is Corporal Ibe?

Okoro: He was on afternoon shift, sir.

D.P.O.: Tell him to see me in my office immediately he resumes duty.

Okoro: Yes Sir! (*The D.P.O. walks into the second door representing his office. Sergeant Okoro walks out of the platform. Coporal Salam starts flipping through the files again.*)

(Snooze)

ACT THREE

Light comes on stage and we see the courtroom. Everybody is already seated. Enter the Judge.

Clerk: Court! (*Everybody in the courtroom stands up. The judge comes in through the door beside his bench and takes his seat. Everybody sits down again.*) Suit number HOL/27P/1989. The State versus Obi Ibe, A Ayinde, and P. Salam.

Judge: Is the prosecuting counsel present?

Barrister Femi: (*Stands up*) Yes, my lord.

Judge: You are Barrister Femi?

Barrister Femi: Yes, my lord. (*sits down.*)

Judge: I hope the defence counsel is also present?

Barrister Ade: Yes, your lordship.

Judge: The prosecuting counsel may now present his case.

Barrister Femi: My lord, after the last hearing I went to the scene of the incident to find out the truth about what happened. And I was able to gather that the accused, Corporal Obi Ibe shot the two deceased persons intentionally. Perhaps he shot his victims out of sheer wickedness and hatred. I also gathered that the mob at the riot scene never attacked the accused. And that the wounds he claimed to have sustained at

30

the scene of the riot were injuries he inflicted on himself with a cigarette fire all with the intention of making his fabricated attack seem real.

Judge: Does the defence counsel have anything to say in relation to this?

Barrister Ade: Yes, your lordship. (*pauses*) I still maintain that Corporal Obi Ibe did not shoot the two deceased persons - Olu and Yemi - intentionally. And my lord, the injuries on Mr. Obi Ibe's body as can be seen in the picture, do not look like injuries created with cigarette fire. My lord, I am sure an injury sustained through a cigarette fire does not bleed as profusely as the injury we see on Obi Ibe's body in the picture. My lord, as I have said earlier, the accused, Corporal Obi Ibe did not shoot the deceased persons intentionally. (*Sits down*).

Judge: Over to the prosecuting counsel. (*Barrister Femi stands up again*).

Barrister Femi: My Lord, I will like to beg the court to permit me to cross–examine the accused before presenting my witnesses.

Judge: You can go ahead.

Barrister Femi: Corporal Obi Ibe, you said the mob that gathered at the scene of the riot attacked you?

Obi Ibe: Yes.

Barrister Femi: Please, would you tell this honourable court the kind of weapons that were used in the attack?

Obi Ibe: Em! Emu … they …

31

Barrister Ade: Objection, my lord. My …

Judge: Objection overruled. The accused should answer the question.

Obi Ibe: They attacked me with firewoods and sticks.

Barrister Femi: (*turns to the judge*) My lord, as an experienced lawyer, I've stood for so many cases of fights and injuries. And since all that while I have never seen a firewood and stick injury appear like bleeding chicken pox. My lord, I put it to the accused that he is a wicked liar. (*The judge notes something down while Barrister Femi sits down.*)

Judge: Does the defence counsel have anything to say about this?

Barrister Ade: My lord, he was actually stabbed with the firewoods and sticks and how I wish the whole injury had not all healed, I would have asked him to show you the fat wounds he sustained from the firewood attack. (*pauses.*) My lord, to actually prove that all what I have so far said are true, I will like to call up a witness to the witness box.

Judge: You can go ahead.

Barrister Ade: (*Signals to Oluwasegun who climbs into the witness box and stands. The Clerk stands up and walks towards him. He presents the Holy Bible and the Holy Qu'ran to Oluwasegun.*)

Clerk: Are you a Christian or a Muslim?

Oluwasegun: I'm a Muslim. (*He hands him the Qu'ran.*)

32

Clerk: Now, say after me. (*pauses.*) In the name of the Almighty Allah … (*Oluwasegun repeats after him as he says the wording of the oath. turns to the judge.*) My lord, the witness is on oath.

Judge: Okay, the defence counsel may now proceed. (*Barrister Ade stands up*)

Barrister Ade: As your lordship pleases. (*pauses.*) Mr Oluwasegun, please, tell this honourable court your full name.

Oluwasegun: My name is Mr. Oluwasegun Aremu Akiwande.

Barrister Ade: What do you do for a living?

Oluwasegun: I am a mechanic.

Barrister Ade: Where is your shop or site located?

Oluwasegun: At Obalende junction.

Barrister Ade: Were you there when the riot started?

Oluwasegun: Yes.

Barrister Ade: Please, tell the court how it all started.

Judge: Mr Oluwasegun, how did you happen to be there?

Barrister Ade: My lord, the riot actually happened at Obalende junction, the same place where his shop is located.

Judge: Okay, you may proceed.

Oluwasegun: The whole incident started when a driver refused the orders of a police *yellow fever* that was controlling the traffic on the junction of the overcrowded road. He accidentally hit another car which the police *yellow fever* ordered to move. While the two drivers started arguing among themselves claiming that each one of them was right, the one whose fault it was attacked the police *yellow fever*, as he told them to drive their cars out of the major road, claiming that the police *yellow fever* caused the accident.

Barrister Ade: It is okay. Tell the court how the policeman beside you (*points at Obi Ibe*) came to be involved.

Oluwasegun: Em ... when the driver started beating the police *yellow fever*, policemen emerged. The rioters wanted to attack them so one of the policemen shot two of them.

Barrister Ade: Did he actually shoot them when they were trying   to attack him or was it when they were beating him?

Oluwasegun: Not really, he was trying to run away and mistakenly his gun shot and the two young men among the rioters fell and died.

Barrister Ade: Mr. Oluwasegun but the accused told me that he was about shooting into the air with the intention of scaring the crowd away when the bullet landed on the deceased persons' chests.

Oluwasegun: Yes, it is exactly.

Judge: The prosecuting counsel, do you have any cross-examination?

Barrister Femi: Yes, my lord.

Judge: You can go ahead.

34

Barrister Femi: As your lordship pleases. (*pauses.*) Mister, what did you say your name is again?

Oluwasegun: My name is Oluwasegun Aremu Akiwande.

Barrister Femi: Do you know the accused?

Oluwasegun: Yes, I mean no— I am just saw him on the riot day and today.

Barrister Femi: Which one do you mean?

Oluwasegun: Em ... No, my lord.

Barrister Femi: Then, what is your *locus-standi*?

Oluwasegun: Em ... Em ... NN.

Barrister Femi: I asked a question.

Oluwasegun: My lord, I don't know what you mean by that.

Barrister Femi: Is that so? (*pauses*) I mean, what connection or what is the reason you have come to stand as a witness for the accused?

Barrister Ade: Objection, my lord ...

Judge: Objection overruled. The witness should answer the question.

Oluwasegun: It is because ... because ... I ... I ... saw the whole thing happen.

Barrister Femi: So what you mean is that you just developed interest in this case.

Oluwasegun: No, my lord!

Barrister Femi: Why have you come to give witness in court?

Oluwasegun: (*starts shivering*) Em … em …

Barrister Ade: Objection, my lord. My learned colleague is probing the witness beyond the basis of this case.

Judge: Objection overruled. His *locus-standi* makes his narration believable or unbelievable. So the prosecuting counsel may proceed.

Barrister Femi: As your lordship pleases.

Oluwasegun: I have said it before.

Barrister Femi: What did you say?

Oluwasegun: It is because I saw the whole thing happen.

Barrister Femi: How did you know this case is on?

Oluwasegun: Em … It … It.

Barrister Ade: Objection …

Judge: Objection overruled

Barrister Femi: Answer the question, Mr Oluwasegun.

Oluwasegun: It was Barrister Ade who said I should come and stand as witness in court.

Barrister Femi: My lord, I put it to Mr. Oluwasegun that he was bribed to come and fabricate this story.

Barrister Ade: Objection my lord.

Judge: Objection overruled. Barrister, please proceed with the cross-examination.

Barrister Femi: As your lordship pleases (*pauses.*) My lord, I am done with the cross-examination but in place of this witness, I beg the court to permit me to invite one of Corporal Obi Ibe's colleagues, Corporal Ayinde, as witness.

Judge: The prosecuting counsel may proceed. (*Ayinde walks up to the witness box while Mr. Oluwasegun is asked to return to the gallery. The Clerk quickly stands up and walks up to the witness box.*)

Clerk: Are you a Christian or a Muslim?

Ayinde: I no be any

Clerk: What is your religion?

Ayinde: I be traditionalist.

Clerk: What exactly do you believe in?

Ayinde: I dey worship Sango.

Clerk: (*puts aside his Holy Bible and his Holy Qu'ran.*) We don't have Sango here but you have to condition your mind as if you are in its presence. (*He leads him through the wordings of the oath and thenturns to the judge.*) My lord, the witness is on oath.

Judge: Okay, the prosecuting counsel may now proceed.

Barrister Femi: As your lordship pleases. (*pauses*) Corporal Ayinde, please tell this honourable court your full name.

Ayinde: My name na Ayinde Abinbola.

Barrister Femi: What is your occupation?

Ayinde: I be policeman.

Barrister Femi: Do you know the other two accused persons standing there?

Ayinde: Yes. Dem be my colleagues

Barrister Femi: Do you know why the three of you are here?

Ayinde: Yes.

Barrister Femi: Please, tell the court why you think you are here and how it all happened.

Ayinde: We dey here because of the shooting of the two boys.That day, me and Corporal Salam dey for station when Obi Ibe come come for inside station with one young man wey him say him rescue from the people way wan burn am because say him stole some amount of moni from one trader....(*light suddenly dims. The light returns again on stage. Enter Corporal Ayinde, Corporal Salam, Sergeant Okoro and two other policemen. They position themselves at the back of the counter. Enter Corporal Obi Ibe with a young man whom he holds so tight on his trousers-belt.*

Obi Ibe: Move! Move! (*Hits the man with the base of his rifle and slaps his head.*) Move, thief! Move! Instead wey you go die there and your dead-body go disturb the neighbourhood, e better make you rotin for cell. (*Almost immediately, a young man runs into the station. The four policemen beside the counter quickly take cover. Corporal Obi Ibe quickly raises his rifle and is ready to shoot.*)

Ayinde: Who be that? (*Still under cover.*)

Obi Ibe: Who be you? Else, I shoot you.

The Young man: (*Panting*) They are beating a policeman at the junction.

Salam: (*Stands up from his hideout*) Which people are beating the policeman? Armed robbers?

The Young man: No! (*Still panting*) They are beating a *yellow fever.*

Obi Ibe: Say na policeman or *yellow fever?*

The Youngman: A police *yellow fever*, officer. (*The policemen gasp*)

Okoro: Why did you *rand* into the station as if an armed robber was chasing you?

The Young Man: I am sorry, officer. I just want to be fast so that you can intervene quickly before they kill the police *yellow fever.*

Okoro: Okay, Corporal Salam and Corporal Ayinde, follow him to the scene of the incident.

Ayinde&Salam: Yes sir!

(Corporal Obi Ibe hands over the arrested young man to another corporal beside the counter and follows Corporal Ayinde and Corporal Salam with his rifle. Light dims again and returns to the main stage. We see Ayinde stops talking while still in the witness box.)

Barrister Femi: Do you mean he was not asked to follow you to the scene of the incident before he did?

Ayinde: Yes.

Barrister Femi: You can proceed with the story.

Ayinde: Okay. *(pauses.)* So when we come reach the place, people don gathered there. *(Light dims and comes on again. We see a crowd of people gathered around a traffic policeman and two drivers. Corporal Obi Ibe, Corporal Ayinde and Corporal Salam come in. As soon as they are seen, the crowd makes way for them. Corporal Ayinde and Corporal Salam advise the traffic policeman to return to his duty in mimes. As they are about to leave, a young boy, Olu, laughs and Corporal Obi Ibe quickly looks to his direction.)*

Olu: This police work self. *(Obi Ibe stops and becomes more interested in his statement while Corporal Ayinde and Corporal Salam walk out of the platform with the arrested drivers.)*

Obi Ibe: Wetin happen to the job?

Olu: Who talk to you? *(intending to run away.)*

Obi Ibe: Come back here! *(Olu still going.)* Stop, else I shoot! *(He still tries to run. Corporal Obi Ibe shoots him and he falls down- dead. His brother, Yemi, rushes in)*

Yemi: Ah, my brother! You have killed my brother! *(wants to attack Corporal Obi Ibe. Corporal Obi Ibe releases another bullet and*

40

Yemi falls down. The crowd becomes angry and starts approaching the Corporal. He quickly releases two bullets into the sky and runs out of the platform. The crowd starts rioting; singing fighting songs. Light dims again and returns to the stage. We see Ayinde in the witness box as before.)

Barrister Femi: My lord, that is all I wanted from the witness.

Judge: Okay, the defence counsel may now cross-examine the witness.

Barrister Ade: You said the accused saved a thief from being burnt, before the young man came into the police station to report the incident?

Ayinde: Yes.

Barrister Ade: After which you presented him as somebody who shot the deceased persons for the fun of it.

Barrister Femi: Objection my lord! My learned colleague should go straight to his question.

Judge: Objection upheld. Defence counsel re-direct your question.

Barrister Ade: As your lordship pleases. Corporal Ayinde, you said he shot the first deceased boy, after you had taken the arrested drivers away, because he made a mere utterance?

Ayinde: Yes.

Barrister Nkeiru: So how did you know that was what happened?

Ayinde: I ...I ...

Barrister Ade: (*cuts in*) My lord, Corporal Ayinde has been bribed to fabricate false story against his colleague, Obi Ibe. My lord, it is not also true that any reasonable man would shoot anybody because of a mere utterance and Obi Ibe is a reasonable man.

Judge: The prosecuting counsel can further present his case.

Barrister Femi: As your lordship pleases. My lord, may I use this opportunity to invite my second witness.

Judge: Go on. (*Barrister Femi signals to Corporal Salam and he walks up to the witness box. The Clerk walks to the witness box while Corporal Ayinde step aside. Corporal Salam is made to make a verbal oath.*)

Clerk: My lord, the witness is on oath. (*Collects the Holy Qu'ran and returns to his seat.*)

Judge: The prosecuting counsel may now proceed.

Barrister Femi: As your lordship pleases. (*pauses.*) Please, tell the court your name.

Salam: My name na Corporal Salam Abdulahi.

Barrister Femi: Do you know this young man? (*points*) I mean Corporal Obi Ibe.

Salam: Yes, my lord.

Barrister Femi: Tell the court your relationship with him.

Salam: He is my colleague. It is with am, Corporal Ayinde and I wentto the place.

Barrister Femi: We have been told the story about how Corporal Obi Ibe killed...

Barrister Ade: Objection, my lord! My learned colleague is forcing the witness to give false evidence.

Judge: Objection upheld. The prosecuting counsel should rephrase the question.

Barrister Femi: As your lordship pleases. (*pauses and then continues.*) We have been told the story about how the accused shot the deceased; we want you to affirm if what Corporal Ayinde said is true.

Salam: Yes, what Corporal Ayinde said na the truth.

Barrister Femi: Tell the court if the crowd attacked you, when you all got to the scene of the riot.

Salam: My lord, the crowd no attack us when we got there. In fact, the two drivers followed us immediately we told them that they are under arrest.

Barrister Femi: How come the accused shot his victims?

Salam: He shot the first boy because he said something irritating, while the second boy was shot because he wanted to attack him in relation to his brother's death.

Barrister Femi: What do you have to say about the wounds on Corporal Obi Ibe's body as evident in the picture he presented to this court?

Salam: Na him inflicted those injuries on himself. Nobody attack us when we reached there.

Barrister Femi: My lord, I am done for now.

Judge: Okay, Barrister Femi. Now, over to the defence counsel. (*Barrister Ade stands up.*)

Barrister Ade: My lord, my learned colleague talked these two policemen into giving false evidence against their colleague, Corporal Obi Ibe.

Barrister Femi: But my lord, there is no way I could have done such a thing. As a matter of fact, these men are the accused person's colleagues and have been in detention with him ever since this case started and would not have lied against him.

Barrister Ade: My lord, corporal Obi Ibe told me that he had a quarrel with these colleagues of his yesterday while waiting in detention for this trial. Little wonder my learned colleague used them to give false evidence against him.

Barrister Femi: My lord, this is not so. The accused used to be in good terms with these two men until after the incident. Their problem actually started when the men blamed him for shooting the boys.

Judge: Okay, I feel this case should be adjourned (*He looks into his file and raises his face again*) to the twentieth day of September (*hits the gavel.*)

Clerk: Court! (*Everybody in the courtroom stands up while the judge disappears into the door beside his bench.*)

(Snooze)

ACT FOUR

Light comes on stage and the police station comes alive again. Enter Corporal Salam and Corporal Ayinde.

Salam: Ayinde, that Madam came here again o.

Ayinde: Say you serious? She come even yesterday?

Salam: Yes o! Sergeant Okoro was the person who attended to am. I was just resuming duty when I saw am here, blabbing as usual.

Ayinde: And wetin Sergeant Okoro do?

Salam: He ignored am! And do you know that after talking for a long time and not replied, she walked away.

Ayinde: What about the D.P.O? Wetin the D.P.O talk about am?

Salam: The D.P.O said we should ignore her.

Ayinde: That case na forgone issue. Make the idiot woman go relax her head. I no know why she dey come here everyday. (*Enter Sergeant Okoro.*)

Salam: Morn Sir! (*They Salute Sergeant Okoro and he replies.*)

Okoro: Has the D.P.O. *camed* here?

Salam: Yes Sir, he just came in some minutes ago.

Okoro: Let me quickly attended to something outside.

Salam: Okay Sir, (*Sergeant Okoro walks out of the platform.*)

Salam: Ayinde, when is Ibe resuming duty? The time is far spent (*Enter Corporal Ibe*)

Ayinde: Oh! See am, he don come.

Obi Ibe: How work today?

Salam: Fine! (*Ayinde tries to write something into the register.*)

Obi Ibe: Oga don come?

Salam: Yes, he asked after you. (*Sergeant Okoro returns.*)

Obi Ibe: Morn Sir! (*salutes and Sergeant Okoro replies.*)

Okoro: Welcome!

Obi Ibe: Yes Sir! (*Sergeant Okoro walks out and the D.P.O. comes out from his office. Corporal Ayinde and Corporal Salam salute while standing behind the counter.*)

D.P.O.: Where is Sergeant Okoro? (*Corporal Ayinde quickly turns to him.*)

Ayinde: E dey outside, Sir.

D.P.O.: Call him. (*Corporal Ayinde rushes out of the platform.*) Yes Corporal, I have heard what happened and I am not pleased with the kind of rubbish you, Ayinde and Ibe did at that riot scene yesterday.

Ayinde: We sorry sir. We trying to protect ourselves sir.

D.P.O.: By killing two innocent persons. Just thank your god that the woman is a poor widow, and has no money to prosecute you. (*Enter Sergeant Okoro and Corporal Ayinde.*) That woman must be frustrated into giving up trying to see Ibe. (*Corporal Salam returns to the counter while Sergeant Okoro stands at attention in the presence of the D.P.O.*) Sergeant!

Okoro: Sir!

D.P.O.: I want all of you to do everything under your power to make sure that that woman forget about this matter.

Okoro: What did I do Sir?

D.P.O.: I don't know. Use your brain. Corporal Ibe must be proved innocent. (*returns to his office.*)

Okoro: Okay sir!

(*All of a sudden, D.P.O. rushes out of his office.*)

D.P.O.: The woman has petitioned this police station at the office of the commissioner of police. There is problem. (*They are shocked.*) Where is Sergeant Okoro?

Okoro: I am here.

D.P.O.: Where are those who carried out that assignment?

47

Okoro: (*points*) It were the three of them, Sir.

D.P.O.: I have warned you against speaking terrible grammar.

Okoro: What I say was correct. Dem be "three" and that is *plural*s and the verb "were" is also plural so that is concord.

D.P.O.: Okay! Pull the uniforms of those who went for that assignment and lock them up in the cell. They will be transferred to the headquarters tomorrow.

Okoro: Yes sir! (*turns to Corporals Ibe, Salam and Ayinde*) Remove your clothes

Salam: Please Sir, (*as he removes his uniform*)

Ayinde: (*as he removes his uniform*) Na Corporal Ibe shoot them (*They remove their uniforms on stage and Sergeant Okoro leads them out of the platform.*)

(Snooze)

***

Light comes on stage and we see the court. Everybody is already seated. A warder leads Corporals Obi Ibe, A. Ayinde and P. Salam into the courtroom.

Clerk: Court! (*Everybody in the courtroom stands up. The judge comes in and sits down.*) Suit number HOL/27P/1989. The State versus Obi Ibe, A Ayinde, and P. Salam.

Judge: Does the prosecuting counsel have any new information that would help the court?

Barrister Femi: No, my lord.

Judge: What about the defence counsel?

Barrister Ade: No, my lord.

Judge: Now, my judgment. (*adjusts his spectacle.*) Corporal Ayinde and Corporal Salam are innocent of the charges against them and are hereby acquitted. And pursuant to section * 101, sub-section *35 and section *751 of the criminal code of The Federal Republic, this court finds Corporal Obi Ibe guilty of the charges levelled against him and he is therefore sentenced to death by hanging. (*There is a shout at the gallery.*)

Clerk: Order!

Judge: Let this be a warning to all policemen. It is wrong to shoot at people merely because they made utterances. And for coming to give a false witness to this honourable court, this court fines Mr Oluwasegun the sum of fifty thousand naira or with the option of serving a three-month jail term. (*hits his gavel.*)

Clerk: Court! (*Everybody in the courtroom stands up. The judge disappears into the door beside his bench. The warder takes Corporal Obi Ibe out as he starts crying.*)

The end

The Haunted

CHARACTERS

CHRISTOPHER- a writer.

NGOZI- his girlfriend.

MOTHER EFURU

MOTHER OKWARAMA-Chorus.

JOHNSON

PAUL- Christopher's friends.

PETER

BOY (i)

BOY (ii)-Ngozi's friends.

On a tombstone

Chris: Poet, Prophet, Patriot
Martyred that the letting of his blood
May hasten the birth of the ideal nation.

Bound as we all are to mere dust,
Laying down our lives,
A light and a signpost to the living,
We hope to make an ally of eternity.

Isidore Diala

ACT ONE

A room. A large space with two doors. The space is demarcated with rolls of arranged pots of flowers and within each spaces created by the demarcation is a door. Another screen of flowers decorates the passage of the room to the first door. This represents the building of a standard university hostel.

In the room is a mattress resting on a well-stretched carpet. A table, having some books and a lamp on it, is seen at the other corner. A chair leans on the table while a stand-fan stands opposite the mattress. A roll of well-arranged books stretches from the corner of the mattress to the end of the wall.

Under a faint blaze of light, we see Mother Efuru and Mother Okwarama in their white robes. Their faces and bodies are painted white. They represent the muses.

The faint-light moves a bit and we see Christopher in his house wears of a white T-shirt and black short-trousers and seated like a statue on the chair. He leans his left hand on the table and stamps it upon his jaw like someone soaked in an ocean of great thought. The light blazes the stage and the scene opens.

Chorus: Christopher! Stop it! You are tormenting your soul! This kind of thought yields nothing; bring your soul together. *(Christopher ignores them, hisses and replaces his left hand with the right one and holds it firmly to his jaw again.)* Remember, art has its own commandments and one of these commandments is that you must not serve two gods.

Christopher: (*glances at them and lowers his face again.*) It's not easy to forget... but I've thought change could be achieved by persistence. (*replaces his left hand with the right one, looks up at the muses and frowns.*)

Chorus: Sure! Change could indeed be achieved by persistence but mind you, a change with a gullible heart. (*Christopher looks more depressed. His face falls and tears drip from his eyes.*) Christopher, give yourself totally to art. Look, art does not smother a man's heart; neither does it smother a man's thought. It gives to a man his thought in its black and white. The best place to work change is in art and not in change itself because change sometimes conceives a marble heart.

Christopher: (*raises his face again.*) Marble heart? (*pauses.*) But change is gradual. That's the reason I don't want to take change with force. That's why I toiled at change with a petting hand. (*pauses.*) But is that why I couldn't change her? Is that why? (*tears drop again and again.*)

Chorus: Christopher, an artist does not work change on himself.

Christopher: But that's not the situation. The truth is that I want to transform her. I want to give her the mind of an artist. So you now can see my reason.

Chorus: Too poor! (*barks*) What reason does reason has over reason? You are only practising art on a sandy ground- art that a drizzle from the sky would forever erase.

Christopher: Do you mean nothing really changes? Not even the mind of an individual could be changed? Is that what you mean? Yes! Tell me! Is that?

55

Chorus: No! Christopher, change will come when it will come. Change is the will of the changed. Change is the decree of the spiritual.

Christopher: *(cuts them short.)* Then why didn't you change her? *(weeping.)* Or would you say it's not art? But art aims more at transformation. Art is to correct errors. Isn't that true? Isn't it? Tell me!

Chorus: Christopher! No! This is not how to achieve change. You do not work change on yourself. Change is kept in the mind and directed at a gullible mind.

Christopher: Gullibility again! *(pauses.)* Is she not a girl? Girls are known for their gullibility.

Chorus: Christopher, but change has developed a marble heart at gullibility. If it is not so, you would not have heard what you heard.

Christopher: How sure are we? You never can judge. Men tell lies sometimes.

Chorus: The world cannot be wrong. Take it for sure that change has developed a marble heart at gullibility.

Christopher: *(bursts into a loud cry.)* It can't be! No! Hers can't be different! *(Enter Johnson from the first door. He overhears a cry.)* No *(Johnson stops and listens again.)* It just can't be! *(Johnson walks on and stops in front of the door.)* No! *(Johnson knocks.)* Why should it be like that? Why? *(Johnsonknocks again. Christopher stops crying. He rubs off the trails of tears on his cheeks and adjusts himself.)* Who is that?

Johnson: It's me! (*still at the door*)

Christopher: Who're you? Don't you have a name?

Johnson: It's Johnson Okoro!

Christopher: Johnson?

Johnson: Yes!

Christopher: Okay, wait for me! (*stands up from the chair and walks to the door. He grabs the bolt, zips it to the right and opens the door.*) Johnson. Have you come? (*Johnson comes in and Mother Efuru and Mother Okwarama make themselves invisible. Johnson walks up to the mattress and sits down.*)

Johnson: I overheard you crying. What was the problem? (*Christopher ignores him.*) I hope you're not into that madness of yours again. So, from soliloquies, it has ascended to crying aloud.

Christopher: No! I don't soliloquize.

Johnson: You would never agree that you ever soliloquize. Would you also say that you were not crying earlier before now? (*no response.*) Answer me, Christopher! Answer me!

Christopher: Okay, (*nonchalantly.*) I was! Any more questions? (*Johnson is dumbfounded.*) Yes! Since we started our life with a cry, we'll continue to cry until that fateful day that we would laugh eternally. So you see, crying is not a crime. It is merely the way of nature. I'll not be the one who would defile the law by not crying now and perhaps cry when I might have crossed the bridge of the living to that of the ancestral.

Johnson: Yes! You are right but something stimulates cry. Even when a child is born, he cries out of the stimulus of some pains. And a mature man also cries out of the stimulus of a pain that has so engulfed his heart. So what was the problem? Why were you crying?

Christopher: *(gasps)* I overheard that Ngozi is dating another boy. In fact the fellow who told me said he saw the boy holding her to himself. *(pauses)* You see, Ngozi whom I love; Ngozi whom I cared for: Ngozi whom I gave all my heart, all my soul, oh Ngozi! *(shakes his head)*

Johnson: I've told you that that girl is not your kind; forget her. If you keep thinking about her you'll only end up killing yourself. See let me tell you, even if you give her the meat of a lion she would not change. *(pauses.)* I've told you that that girl is a harlot.

Christopher: *(upset)* Stop it! *(groans.)* But I've told you that she isn't a harlot. She is only rough. Roughness isn't harlotry. But why did you call her that in my presence again? Why? You want to upset me. Isn't it?

Johnson: *(frowns.)* Why are you supporting her? Somebody who hurts you every second and every minute.... Are you out of your mind? *(pauses)* I didn't want to tell you, but let me tell you now. I saw her as I was coming to your house...

Christopher: *(cuts in.)* Really? Was she coming here?

Johnson: If she were, it would have been better.

Christopher: Why didn't you call her then?

Johnson: You need to know the state I saw her in.

Christopher: (*frowns*) In what state did you see her in?

Johnson: I saw her with a boy. They were at a corner, talking and the boy was mesmerizing her. (*Christopher is almost going to faint.*)

Christopher: Are they still there now?

Johnson: Probably. (*Christopher starts going out.*) Wait! Wait! (*Christopher stops.*) I came to borrow your....

Christopher: (*cuts in.*)Wait till I come back. (*runs out of the room and then out of the first door. Johnson walks towards the roll of arranged books and starts searching for the book he came for. He sees it, picks it up and sits down on the chair. After a while, Christopher returns. He opens the door and enters the room.*) I didn't see her. Are you sure of what you said?

Johnson: You see, that's the reason I don't like telling you anything.

Christopher: (*still boiling*) In what wears did you see her?

Johnson: (*upset*) So you still don't believe that I saw her? (*Stands up and makes a move to go out.*) Well, I've collected the book I came for?

Christopher: No! (*stops him*) Not like that! I merely wanted to know the kind of wears she was waaring so that I could know how to follow her up when she comes.

Johnson: Oh! You want to tell her that I saw her?

Christopher: No! Why would I?

Johnson: Okay, what are you going to tell her?

Christopher: Don't bother yourself; I'm not a small boy. I can handle her. (*touches him on his chest.*) Don't worry about that at all!

Johnson: Okay, she was in a black tight trousers and a half blouse that covered her body up to the stomach. And her belly was revealed to the world. (*Disgusted.*) In fact when I saw her, she irritated me. I pretended as if, I never knew her. (*upset*) In fact, Christopher, quit that girl. She is not your match. Look for a better girl. Good girls are everywhere on campus. I don't know what you saw in that prostitute.

Christopher: This is growing into an insult. (*turns his face away.*) I can't tolerate this. (*pauses.*) Ngozi is not a prostitute; neither is she a harlot, so stop it.

Johnson: I'm only advising you. You're my friend, a very close friend. You're like a brother to me. (*pauses.*) How would I like to open my eyes and watch you ruined by a mere girl? How would I? Tell me! How would I, Christopher, tell me? Tell me that you would be happy if you were in my shoes. Stare into my eyes and tell me how happy you would be, Christopher! Tell me! (*holds him.*) Tell me!

Christopher: I'm not against the fact that you say your mind. I'm only against the names you call her. (*walks back to his chair and sits down.*) Come and sit down. Why are you in a hurry? Come and sit down.

Johnson: (*unwilling*) I have assignments to do in my hostel.

Christopher: No, just for a little chat. Come! You have the whole of tomorrow, being Sunday to do them. You also have this evening and night to yourself. So, sit down let's chat. Sit down! *(Johnson sits down and crosses his legs.)* Johnson, you know I love you. I love your advice. Do you know that among all my friends you are the one I rated first and not only first but most important? Do you know?

Johnson: I haven't known this until now. *(smiles and then shrugs.)* Yes, if you don't like me, who would you? After all, my advice is to make you rob out that dried-leaf love she used in blindfolding you so that you can see what you are doing to yourself.

Christopher: In fact that is why I love you.

Johnson: Who will abhor he who shows him the way to life? Anybody who does that is a big *(in a high tone)* fool!

Christopher: So Johnson, please describe the boy whom you saw her with.

Johnson: So you are at this again. *(pauses and frowns.)* Or you didn't believe me?

Christopher: No! I believe you but I just want enough facts to use to hold her down.

Johnson: Is the fact that she is promiscuous not enough to discard her?

Christopher: No! I've not really caught her .You know I've to prove to her that I saw her myself by telling her the look of the young man you saw her with. *(pauses)* Or is he an old man?

Johnson: No*! (almost bursting into laughter.)* How can he be an old man? It was a boy, a handsome boy. He was wearing a neat white T-shirt and a baggy jeans and on his legs, were big, big shoes - boots *(Christopher groans.)*. And he was holding her *(demonstrating how)* to himself and was caressing her back and…

Christopher: It's enough!

Johnson: No! It's not. Let me complete it.

Christopher: No, it's already complete. I don't want to hear more of it. This one you've said is enough.

Johnson: Wait, I have not told you how she kissed him in the public.

Christopher: *(interested again.)* Ah! Did she kiss him?

Johnson: Yes, she did.

Christopher: No! She didn't. Perhaps, she had only pecked him.

Johnson: But I saw it! I saw it!

Christopher: No! You didn't.

Johnson: I saw it!

Christopher: Then what were you looking at before you saw them?

Johnson: You still ask questions? At them, of course.

Christopher: And you looked at them for a very long time and they didn't see you?

Johnson: No o! It was exactly the time I passed, I saw her kiss him.

Christopher: What of the caress you talked about?

Johnson: Yes, I saw them and she blessed him with a kiss.

Christopher: *(upset.)* No! Not a kiss!

Johnson: It's a kiss!

Christopher: Not a kiss!

Johnson: It is!

Christopher: Not!

Johnson: It is!

Christopher: It is not.

Johnson: Okay, suit yourself. I should tell you what I saw and not the other way round.

Christopher: It seems sometimes you don't see well.

Johnson: So, you're bringing insult into this.

Christopher: No! It's not an insult at all. *(pauses.)* But Johnson, were you putting on your glasses when you saw them?

Johnson: I hope you've not started the insult proper.

Christopher: No! No! How would I? I just want to know.

Johnson: Okay, did you see me with any spectacle? I said I saw her with the boy when I was coming to your house.

Christopher: Oh! Oh! Oh! You were not with your glasses. (*Excited*) Then you are not sure.

Johnson: You see, I know you want to insult me. *(stands up.)*

Christopher: What are you doing?

Johnson: I'm going.

Christopher: Going where?

Johnson: Home, of course!

Christopher: Please stay for a while. At least for a little more chat.

Johnson: Unless you'll say a new thing. If it's your Ngozi talk, I'm tired of it.

Christopher: Okay, we'll discuss new things. Do you hear? (*Johnson nods his head*) Okay, sit down. (*He sits down again*)

Johnson: Yes! (*remembers something.*) Have you finished editing that novel?

Christopher: Which one?

Johnson: The one you entitled The Adventurer's Mind?

Christopher: Oh! The Adventurer's Mind? (*Johnson nods his head delightfully.*) I'm through with it. I'm cooking a classical play now. You need to read it. It's so powerful. In fact, it has a heart. It breathes. (*brings out a file, flips through it*).

64

Johnson: (*impatiently*) What is the title? What?

Christopher: (*brings out the manuscript and reads out the title page.*) The face of the haunted.

Johnson: The face of the haunted? (*stands up, walks towards him.*) Let me see. (*Christopher extends it to him. He collects it and returns to the mattress. He sits on it and folds his legs. Flips through the manuscripts.*) I guess this one would be interesting also. (*turns to Christopher.*) I enjoyed that, The Adventurer's Mind. I enjoyed most the way you ended the story. I had thought the boy would later marry the harlot. But the way the boy came to meet with the harlot's other friends and the way the girl was put to shame at the end is a lesson that our girls of nowadays should learn. (*pauses.*) Has Ngozi gone through that work?

Christopher: Yes! She has. She said she loves the way the story ended. She even called woe upon the harlot in the work.

Johnson: Really?

Christopher: Yes! (*pauses.*) Yes, let me tell you something about that story.

Johnson: Tell me! What is it? (*Christopher walks close to him and squats before him.*)

Christopher: Do you know, I wrote it only as a piece of advice to her?

Johnson: Really?

Christopher: But only to my surprise, she read it and found it fascinating. That's why I said she has changed. That's why I said I've succeeded in changing her with art. (*pauses.*) Johnson,

65

do you know that art is powerful? Do you know that art is wonderful? Do you know that art can turn black to white? Do you know?

Johnson: Yes I know. Art is powerful, wonderful and all, only to those who know its worth. And you said she has changed? If she has changed, she wouldn't be in that corner with the boy I saw her with.

Christopher: *(confused.)* But…But… She said she has changed.

Johnson: Oh! Oh! Oh! *(laughs.)* I thought you observed it yourself. I never knew she was speaking through you. *(Christopher stands up and turns to his desk. All of a sudden, some voices are heard from the outside. Two boys enter from the second door. They are dressed in jean trousers and boot shoes.)*

Boy (1): You see that babe, dem say na any how O. Me I don cut my own share from her body. *(smiles.)*

Boy (11): The babe fine o. How you use get am now? *(Johnson stops Christopher with a wave of his hand. And they pay more attention to what the boys are saying.)*

Boy (1): I just try my luck and all of a sudden she just fall for my trap and you trust me now, I just smash am at once. *(Johnson stands up from the mattress and tiptoes to the door. He peeps through the keyhole. And suddenly he grips his head and beckons to Christopher. Christopher quickly tiptoes to the door.)*

Johnson: That is the boy whom I saw Ngozi with.

Christopher: Really! *(Johnson still peeps)* Let me see him. *(urging him off the keyhole.)* Let me see him! *(Johnson goes out of the door and*

66

Christopher replaces him.) There are two boys there, talking, which of them do you mean?

Johnson: *(replies from behind)* I mean the one in white T-shirt, blue jean trousers and brown boots and not the other who is in black T-shirt, blue jean trousers and black boots. *(pauses)* Okay, let me see them again. *(Christopher refuses to permit him and keeps peeping)*

Boy (I): She say make I wait for am here by ten o'clock and… *(glances at his wristwatch.)* It's past ten. Say another person never carry am go?

Boy (II): *(laughs.)* You never can say o, you know girls now. Person no fit trust them. That particular time wey dem dey with you na e be the time wey dem be your friend o. So no put your mind too much say she go come. *(Christopher boils. He becomes restless and then goes back to his chair. Johnson quickly replaces him, starts peeping through the keyhole again and later returns to Christopher.)*

Johnson: Christopher, you look depressed?

Christopher: It seems they are talking about Ngozi or what do you think?

Johnson: That's what I think because I'm sure it is that boy I saw her with.

Christopher: *(rests his head on the table, bittered. After a while he raises it again.)* No! *(shakes his head)* It's not Ngozi. Ngozi has changed. She can't be the person they're talking about.

Johnson: (*upset*) Christopher, you provoke me with your argument- things that you know are true you still argue over them.

Christopher: I'm not saying you are telling lies but I don't think Ngozi would have told the boys to come and wait for her there even when she knew that I might catch a glimpse of her.

Johnson: You see, that is why I'm telling you that she can't change; even if you give her heaven and earth, she would not. Girls of her kind can't be satisfied with one man.

Christopher: Not Ngozi! (*Johnson returns to the keyhole and starts peeping again.*) She told me she has no other friend besides me. (*All of a sudden, Ngozi emerges from the second door. Johnson beckons to Christopher. Before Christopher could peep through the keyhole, the boys have joined her and they are out of sight.*) You see, Johnson, you are deceiving me. I thought you said she came around now.

Johnson: Yes, she did! Look very well. (*Christopher peeps again and is disappointed.*)

Christopher: (*furiously.*) Nothing! Those boys have gone, that's all. I didn't see anything. I didn't (*Johnson urges him out with a little push and peeps through the keyhole himself.*)

Johnson: Oh! They have gone out with her.

Christopher: I know that's what you'll conclude. I know!

Johnson: So you still think I'm telling you lies. (*upset*) Okay, I'm going home. (*opens the door.*)

Christopher: Are you angry? (*Johnson is already going.*)

68

Johnson: No! (*Christopher quickly opens the door to call him back but he is out of the platform. Christopher returns to the room and sits on the chair. Mother Efuru and Mother Okwarama, the muses make themselves visible again.*)

Chorus: I think this is enough to make you remove your mind from her and soak it back into art. (*Christopher stares at them and ignores them. He opens his chest of drawer, brings out an exercise book and places it on the table. He picks up his biro and starts writing – he has been possessed again. Mother Efuru cuts off her thought from Mother Okwarama's and each now holds her individual thought and voice*).

Mother Efuru: I smell danger!

Mother Okwarama: I see a god coming down to take up the same role he could have perfectly assigned to a character.

Mother Efuru: Love will also die.(*Light becomes faint again and blazes upon the muses and from them it moves upon Christopher and we see him moving his biro with great vim and in full concentration. His face is covered with sweat. He stands up, walks to his door, picks up his towel and rubs off the streaming sweat and then goes back to his chair. He sits on his stool, picks up his biro and continues writing. After that while the light disappears.*)

(Snooze)

ACT TWO

A faint light returns on stage. In the room, the faint light comes on the wall and reveals a ticking wall clock. The wall clock can be heard ticking aloud from the platform. The light increases a little and we see the long hand of the clock resting on the number two while the short hand points at the number one. The light returns to its usual faint manner and moves out from the wall, only to blaze on Christopher. We see him, sweating under the full grip of his biro. After a while, he stands up, stretches out himself and yawns, with the biro still in his hand. He drops his hand on the table and releases the biro from the clasp grip of his fingers. He stands up from his chair, walks towards his door, then picks up his towel and rubs off his sweat. Suddenly, he feels something in his stomach. He quickly collects some folds of toilet paper, opens his door, comes out to the veranda, and walks out through the first door. The light returns in a full vim and blazes on the stage again. Enter Ngozi with boy (1) from the first door. They stop immediately after coming in. We see Ngozi signals to him to start going back and that she will see him later. Boy (1) nods and moves close to her. She becomes worried. She asks him why, by spreading out her hands and he signals that he wants to peck her. She quickly gives him her cheek to do it. He pecks her and is satisfied. She bids him 'bye' and he reciprocates it. He turns back and starts going out. Then enter Christopher. They hit themselves and each says 'sorry' to the other. Boy (1) walks out of the stage. Christopher stops and looks out through the door, to see him properly. He returns to Ngozi. Ngozi quickly cheers up. She grabs him by his waist and urges him on to his door. They open the door and enter. Ngozi jumps upon the bed and Christopher returns to his chair.

Christopher: Ngozi, who was that boy?

71

Ngozi: *(smiles, gets up from the bed and walks towards Christopher.)* That boy?

Christopher: Yes, that boy? *(She grabs Christopher by his cheeks, kisses him and starts dragging him towards the bed.)* No! Tell me who that boy was first! *(pauses)* Who was that boy who bade you bye, before I came in?

Ngozi: *(furious.)* Is that why you will not follow me to the bed? *(releases her hands and folds them across her breasts)*

Christopher: Who was that boy?

Ngozi: I don't like that question!

Christopher: That's not what I'm asking you; I want to know who that boy was. *(pauses.)* Now, who was that boy? *(furiously.)*

Ngozi: *(returns to the bed, sits down and frowns)* He was asking me after somebody and I told him that nobody like that stays here, then he left.

Christopher: *(frowns.)* Then why must you bid him bye?

Ngozi: He first bade me bye, and I reciprocated it. Is anything wrong with that?

Christopher: Ngozi, you're telling me lies. It can't be.

Ngozi: I can't tell you something and you believe me unless the ones other people tell you. If you know you are no longer interested in this relationship, tell me; I would only think of it for a while and forget it.

Christopher:(*dumbfounded. turns away from Ngozi and faces the work on his table. He picks up his biro and starts writing and suddenly Mother Efuru and Mother Okwarama resume their work*). Okay! (*shrugs*).

Chorus: Christopher, art preserves time.

Christopher: Don't worry; I must finish this work today.

Ngozi: (*cuts in.*) You've started again. I've told you that I don't like you soliloquizing whenever I'm with you.

Christopher: I'm not soliloquizing!

Ngozi: Maybe it's this thing you write all the time that makes you do it.

Christopher: But I'm not soliloquizing.

Ngozi: I'm not expecting you to say you were. (*stands up from the bed and walks majestically to him*). It seems you will stop writing now. I want you to give me your attention. I deserve it and I want it. It is not when I come here you abandon me for your stupid books.

Christopher: No! They aren't stupid. Don't call them stupid. Please, watch your tongue.

Ngozi: Even at that, stop writing for now. Stop it. (*collects his biro. Christopher stands up from his seat and starts groping for the biro.*)

Christopher: (*angry now.*) Ngozi! (*stops struggling.*) Would you give me that biro now? Would you?

Ngozi: I won't! (*positions the biro at her back.*) Beat me. Beat me! I'll never give it to you.

Christopher: (*boils.*) I say give me the biro.

Ngozi: I'll not! (*shrugs.*) Beat me! Kill me! I want to die in your hands. Kill me!

Christopher: (*walks close to her.*) Give me the biro! I will beat you o!

Ngozi: That is what I want. Beat me! (*stretches out her hand and collects the book from the table.*) I've collected this one also; so now, beat me.

Christopher: (*shivers like one under spiritual attack. He grabs her by her neck and positions his hand as if he is to blow her on the face.*) Give me!

Chorus: Christopher! No! (*Christopher holds his peace.*) The beauty of art is that it gives life. (*Ngozi senses the quietness in him and quickly hits him on his chest.*)

Ngozi: Beat me! I thought you said you are going to beat me. Why are you putting down your hand? Beat me, let me see. Just let your hands touch me and see if I will not break your head with... with... (*Her eyes creeps on to the wall clock and stops there*)... with that wall clock.

Christopher: Please, give me that book.

Ngozi: But I said I'm not giving it to you.

Christopher: Ngozi, please give me. This is the only time I have to create that soul.

Ngozi: Which soul?

Christopher: That book you are holding.

Ngozi: This book? *(looks at the book.)*

Christopher: Yes! That book! *(pauses.)* It's immortal. Give it to me, so that I can give it a good set of eyes, a good set of ears. A good nose and mouth and finally a good figure so that everyman can admire it and seek for it just as men seek for beautiful women.

Ngozi: This book? *(amazed.)* The way you talk sometimes makes me angry. How can you be talking about beautifying a book by writing this thing you called story in it?

Christopher: Don't bother, you will not understand. *(pauses.)* Please, let me have it. *(She gives him both the book and the biro.)*

Ngozi: But Christopher, why is it that… *(pauses and starts staring into Christopher's eyes. She clears her throat and resumes again.)* Come and sit with me on the bed. *(grabs Christopher by his right hand and pulls him towards herself.)*

Christopher: No! I abhor sitting on the bed most especially when my muses have not approved of it.

Ngozi: You've started this your muse talk again. I've told you that I don't like you talking about it whenever I am around you.

Christopher: I can't stop doing it. My life lies in it. *(pauses.)* I shall not live a worthwhile life if not for them being by my side.

Ngozi: Okay, I've heard you. Just come and sit with me.

Christopher: But I said no!

Ngozi: Come now! (*Christopher refuses.Silence.*) Okay, you will not sit for too long. I just want to ask you something after which you'll return to your chair and continue writing since you've vowed that your biro would kill you. (*Christopher laughs and then follows her in to the bed. She sits down and leans on the wall. Christopher bends down and sits in the bed, backing the opposite wall. She stares into Christopher's eyes. Christopher returns it with his own look. They both smile. She collects Christopher's left hand and places it on herself.*) Christopher!

Christopher: Yes!

Ngozi: Why is it that you don't give me attention?

Christopher: Ngozi! (*pauses.*)

Ngozi: I'm listening.

Christopher: I don't know the kind of attention you need. (*He pauses.*) You're my only friend. It was out of my assistance you got your O level. I was the one who bought JAMB form for you and I also accompanied you for the exam. (*pauses.*) Ngozi, what kind of attention do you need?

Ngozi: That's not what I am saying.

Christopher: I'm not surprise at what you said. I'm not surprised - that is what women say, when they want to run away from a man.

Ngozi: But ... But ... you... You ...

Christopher: Perhaps, some other boys have been giving you those things you desire. They might have been giving you money. I know you like money so much.

Ngozi: You've started again, Christopher. *(pointing to his face.)* You've started again.

Christopher: I'll not allow you to trick me again. You've tricked me so much. I'll not allow it this time. *(His face changes and falls like that of a bereaved person.)* But what have I done to you, Ngozi? What have I done? Is it wrong loving you? Tell me! *(grabs her by her two hands. tears start dripping from his eyes.)* What have I done to deserve this?

Ngozi: But, why are you crying? What did I do this time again? Why are you crying? *(tries to console him.)*

Christopher: Why must I continue to be hurt? Why is it that you don't bother about me? *(removes her hands and returns to his chair, lowers his head upon his desk and starts weeping aloud. She walks up to him and starts consoling him.)*

Ngozi: Okay, I'm sorry but I haven't done anything O! I'm sorry, if I've hurt you. *(pauses.)* I've always loved you. But... but...

Christopher: But what? *(In between tears.)*

Ngozi: You don't give me attention!

Christopher: *(stops crying all of a sudden. Sits aright and stares into her face.)* How do you mean? What attention?

Ngozi: You don't pet me. You don't give me money. You talk about book, book, and book. You don't take me to party. You don't take me to 'Mr. Biggs'. You don't take me to 'Mr. Fans'. We merely sit in your room and talk of book, book, book. Is it book that I'll eat or will I die on books?

Christopher:*(Astonished.)* No! Ngozi!

Ngozi:I'll say it. It is the truth. I will say my mind.

Christopher: No, Ngozi! This is a very bad thought. This thought would ruin me.*(pauses.)* Please, please, erase it from your mind! *(kneels before her and starts begging her.)* Please, don't say it again. *(pauses. falls to the floor. weeps for a while. Ngozi lowers her head as she sits on the mattress and then stares at him.)*

Ngozi: But Christopher, you are too bookish. You don't have time for yourself talk less of for me.

Christopher: *(stares at her from the floor with dried eyes.)* But you knew these since the past two years or didn't you? Tell me.

Ngozi:*(ignores him and continues again.)*You over labour me with domestic works. Every time I come, you would say *(miming him now)* I want you to go to the market, cook soup for me. I want to eat rice, so cook it for me. *(stares at him now in a straight face and frowns, stands up from the mattress and walks up to the chair. Positions the chair on a comfortable place and sits on it.)* I'm supposed to be served when I come to your house and not me serving you again after taking the pains to come to visit you.

Christopher: No! I'll not do that; I'll not in the cause of changing you ruin you. I want you to reason like an artist. I want to bring you to art; I want to initiate you.

78

Ngozi: Yes! You've started again. Yes, that is another point, how would I be going out with somebody who always talks to himself? Apart from talking to himself, he talks of art all the time someone comes to his house. Instead of us discussing like lovers, he talks about art,   art, and art.

Christopher: It's because art is life; art itself is love; art teaches love everlasting.

Ngozi: (*Aside.*) You see, he doesn't understand, that which you said you don't like is what he capitalizes on, perhaps to get you upset. *(To Christopher.)* But I said I don't like listening to your art talk.

Christopher: *(starts begging her again.)* Please, try to love it because you can't do without it. We can't be together without it. Please, like it for old time's sake.

Ngozi: Old times – okay, do you want me to pay you all that you have spent, so that you will have no need to mention them again?

Christopher: No! You can't afford to pay me, with money. I want you to pay me back with true love; I want you to refrain from boys and to take your studies seriously.

Ngozi: *(returns to the bed and lies down.)* I'm tired of arguing with you. You argue a lot – I don't have your strength. (*There is silence for a while. Christopher rubs off the trail of tears on his cheeks and climbs unto the bed and then sits by her side.)*

Christopher: Ngozi!

Ngozi: What's it again? Let me rest or do you want me to go?

Christopher: No! I don't want you to go. I only want to ask you something.

Ngozi: Okay, what is it?

Christopher: Is it true that a boy was romancing you in a corner? *(Ngozi is shocked. She gathers herself together and sits up.)* Is it true you kissed him? Is it true that he was caressing you? Is it true? *(She composes herself.)*

Ngozi: Did you see me kiss anybody?

Christopher: N...N... *(changes his mind all of a sudden)* Yes! I saw you.

Ngozi: Then why didn't you call me? I know it's all lies. Supposing you saw me you would have called me – I know you well.

Christopher: Ngozi? Why is it that you can't stop this? It was because of this I struggled to get you into this school. I thought you were doing this, because you do nothing, but now that you are a student you ... you ... you ... *(gasped.)*

Nogzi: *(cuts in.)* What did I do? Every time you believe what your friends tell you. Did you see me yourself? Did you? *(Enter Johnson – through the first door. He walks towards Christopher's door and knocks. Christopher is startled. He quickly rubs off the trails of tears on his cheeks with the back of his palm and adjusts himself.)*

Christopher: Who is that? *(another knock.)* Who is knocking?

Johnson: It is I, Johnson.

Christopher: Oh! Johnson *(He stands up from the mattress and walks down to the door. He unzips the door and opens it).* Come in. *(Johnson comes in and walks straight to the chair. He stares at the chair, to see if he can sit on it.)* It's not dirty. Sit on it. *(He sits down and crosses his legs.)*

Johnson: Ngozi, you've come.

Ngozi: Yes! *(pauses.)* How is the going?

Johnson: Not too bad! *(Christopher returns to his former position.)*

Christopher: Johnson, I'm sorry for provoking you then.

Johnson: Don't mention it! *(pauses.)* I came to stay with you. I've been lonely so I felt it's better to come and stay with you. But I hope I'm not disturbing.

Christopher: No! No! You're not; it's good you are here. I was asking her about that place we saw her.

Johnson: Christopher, please, I've not come here to judge or to argue again.

Christopher: I'm not luring you into anything as such; I'm merely asking you after what we saw.

Johnson: Well, that's your business and not mine.

Christopher: I know, but did we not see her?

Johnson: I – we did!

Christopher: But she is denying it. She still insists that she is not the person we saw. *(tears circles in his eyes and starts dripping again.)*

Johnson: So, you're crying because of that? *(to Ngozi.)* But Ngozi why do you do these? You know how much he loves you but you still engage in this shameful act.

Ngozi: But he is lying. He didn't see me. He is merely accusing me.

Johnson: I was with him when he saw you. Even, we saw you kiss the boy. *(pauses.)* Christopher would have burst into your mist but I prevented him. He would have killed you with his hands in the presence of the boy, but ... but ... I ... I ... calmed him down.

Ngozi: But ... But ... *(can't find a word.)*

Christopher:*(rubs off the trail of tears again.)* Any time I get her again, I'll kill her. *(now staring at his hands.)* I'll smother her with my bare hands. I'll grip her so tight on the neck. *(He directs his hands towards her neck and holds it softly.)*

Ngozi: Please, get your hands off my neck.

Chistopher: ... I'll watch her eyes turn upside down. I'll keep my hands still, tight, until gore streams down her nostril and mouth. I'll still hold my hands still; until she falls down and breathes her very last breathe.

Johnson: Ngozi, do you know that, it's painful seeing one's dearest friend misbehaving. If it was me, I'll poison the girl, when she comes to my house and finally throw her away into the school-bush, at midnight. *(Ngozi beams at them.)*

Ngozi: *(to Christopher.)* You think if you kill me my parents would let you go free?

Christopher: So, you'll do it? *(almost going to slap her.)*

Ngozi: *(bends to dodge the slap)* I don't mean to do it.

Johnson: Don't beat her. *(stands up from his seat and holds him by his hand.)* Don't beat her. And if you must beat her, it mustn't be here that I'm with you.

Ngozi: So you want to beat me? *Ngwa!* Beat me let me see. Beat me, and you'll tell me whether you've paid my bride price. Beat me now! *(pushes Johnson behind. Johnson staggers to the chair.)* Let him beat me!

Johnson: Oh! Oh! I was trying to prevent him from beating you and what I got, as my reward was a push.

Ngozi: *(turns to Johnson.)* Johnson, sorry but I want him to beat me. He has been talking about this for a long time. I want him to do it now so that he may rest. *(Christopher hits her softly and she roars like a lioness. She pounds on him, hits him, slaps him and kicks him. Johnson quickly intervenes and stops her.)* Useless boy! Look at his head – like that of a ripe mango. Coward! He is only strong when he sees me.

Christopher: *(boiling now.)* Johnson, wait, let me beat this prostitute to my satisfaction. Just allow me.

Johnson: She is a girl. Don't mind all what she is saying. They have their tongues as their strength, so let her be. I've warned

83

you against all these as a friend but you wouldn't listen, you prefer all this embarrassment.

Ngozi: Johnson! No! Don't bring your own into this. Just don't!

Johnson: What do you mean? I'm only talking to Christopher and not to you.

Ngozi: I just hope it's so.*(frowns. pauses.)* In fact, I'm leaving your room. Maybe that is why you are insulting me. *(sways towards the door.)*

Christopher: Ngozi! Come back here! Come back here, Ngozi! (*She opens the door and walks out. Christopher stands up and rushes towards the door. She quickens her walk and disappears through the first door. Christopher follows her. After a while, Christopher enters again through the same door. He walks to his door, opens it, comes in and zips the bolt again.*)

Johnson: Christopher! Honestly you are taking shit from that girl. If I were in your shoes, I would have done away with her long ago.

Christopher: You don't understand.

Johnson: I don't understand what?

Christopher: You don't understand how love breathes.

Johnson: If I don't, then tell me. *(Enter Paul and Peter. They walk to Christopher's door. Paul takes the lead. He knocks at the door.)*

Christopher: What! (*places his finger across his lips.*) It seems somebody is at the door.

Johnson: Ask the person to come in but that wouldn't stop me from saying what I want to say.

Christopher: *(whispers.)* It seems it is Ngozi.

Johnson: I'm not afraid of her. After all I'm only saying my mind. *(Paul knocks again.)*

Christopher: Okay, come in! *(Paul pushes the door but the door remains still.)* Sorry, wait let me unlock it. *(walks up to the door and unlocks it. Paul and Peter enter, shaking hands with Christopher and Johnson one after the other.)* Sit down, relax and feel comfortable.

Peter: I saw Ngozi going down to her hostel in a straight face; was there any problem? *(Christopher refuses to say anything.)*

Johnson: Yes, she was quarrelling with Christopher.

Paul: *(turns to Christopher.)* You and that your Ngozi self- na wa o!

Christopher: Please, sit down. *(Paul sits on the chair while Peter relaxes on the mattress.)*

Peter: What was the problem this time?

Johnson: It was about promiscuity- her usual game.

Paul: I'm not afraid; monkeys don't forsake the trees.

Christopher: I don't like that talk.

Peter: Johnson?

Johnson: Yes!

Peter: Do you know what pains me most?

Johnson: No!

Peter: Supposing she goes out with boys who have cars or these big-time politicians, it wouldn't have bothered me because that will be enough excuse; at least, I'll say she is after money or car.

Paul: You're correct.

Peter: But instead you see her with boys whom Christopher is far better than.

Paul: Just because they put on jean trousers and one hundred Naira T-shirt. (*They all burst out into laughter – except Christopher who tightens up.*)

Peter: Christopher, you're my friend, I advise you to leave that girl. She is not your match. She is too odd for you. You need to think.

Christopher: Love does not grow in a day. Love is a gradual thing. Love is not rushed.

Paul: I agree with you, Christopher. But mind you, you don't expect a lion to grow love for a sheep.

Christopher: What do you mean?

Paul: The love a lion has for a sheep is of taste and not of brotherliness. That best explains the kind of love Ngozi has for you.

Christopher: No man accepts love into himself for love's sake. Man is compelled to love by external forces.

Johnson: How do you mean? You had once said that love is an external concept and now you are also saying that man is compelled to love by external forces. How do you mean? Is it not better reasoned that man is compelled to love by internal forces?

Christopher: Okay, explain what you mean.

Johnson: A man decides to love and love does not compel man to accept it.

Christopher: You're totally wrong, Johnson. A man neither decides to love nor to hate, but know it that both love and hatred exist outside man – they are external. The decision of hatred or of love, as the case may be, is compelled by the attribute of that which is to be loved or hated. Do you understand?

Johnson: Yes, I was right then! That was what I said.

Christopher: No! That wasn't what you said.

Johnson: It was!

Christopher: It wasn't! Supposing you did I would have said so.

Johnson: But I did.

Christopher: You didn't.

Peter: You've started this mad argument of yours again

Johnson: But I did.

Christopher: No! You didn't.

Paul: It's okay!

Johnson: But I did!

Christopher: You didn't.

Paul: Johnson, you did!

Christopher: But....

Paul: *(cuts in.)* Christopher, honestly, he didn't.

Johnson: What do you mean then?

Paul: I thought I've answered you, why not be calm.

Christopher: I'm only happy that you included "honestly". *(There is silence. Johnson breaks it.)*

Johnson: Let me go and get all my washed clothes inside. I know they must have been dried by now. *(stands up from the mattress and walks out.)*

Christopher: Paul! Yes! Come and see the new work I'm creating.

Paul: What's the title?

Christopher: The face of the haunted.

Paul: The face of the haunted? The title is something else; tell me   something about the story.

Christopher: I'm not a storyteller.

Paul: How do you mean?

Christopher: I'm a writer and not a storyteller.

Paul: Okay! When will you finish the story?

Christopher: This evening will do!

Paul: Will you let me read the story, even at its original draft?

Christopher: Why not. (*pauses.*) But you'll have to promise me that it will be safe because just as you know, it will be my original manuscript.

Paul: It will be safe, I promise.

Christopher: You can come for it at night.

Paul: Promised?

Christopher: Yes! (*Peter stands up and stretches himself.*)

Peter: Paul, lets go.

Christopher: Go where?

Paul: To our room, of course!

Christopher: Paul, I think you have the right to go when you want. Peter mustn't force you along anywhere he goes.

Peter: Look Christopher, everyman is his brother's keeper.

Christopher: Well, it's true. (*Paul and Peter walk out of the platform. Christopher returns to his chair, picks up his biro and continues with his write-up. Mother Efuru and Mother Okwarama resume their work.*)

Chorus: It's high time you accepted what you friends told you.

Christopher: I'll think over it.

Chorus: I see a god die a natural death.

Christopher: Transformation! I need to concentrate to be able to transform her life. Let's focus on transformation first. (*pauses.*) The highest point in art is that period when art successfully transforms human life.

Chorus: Let art do it itself.

Christopher: Art is like a seed that must be planted. Please, let me plant art in a human person.

Chorus: Art withers in he who hates it.

Christopher: Please, let me be, so that I may finish this work tonight.

(Snooze)

ACT THREE

A faint light returns on stage. It creeps to the wall of Christopher's room and reveals the wall-clock. It beams on the wall-clock and we see the short hand pointing at the number seven while the long hand rests on the number twelve. The red thin hand in between the two hands is busy ticking aloud in an alarming speed. The light returns on Christopher who is still on his chair, (bending towards his desk with a biro in his hand) writing on a notebook with a committed spirit. He drops his biro and walks towards the light switch. He presses the switch down with his finger and the bulb snaps and brightens the room. He returns to his desk, picks up his biro and continues writing. After a while, he is done. He walks towards his towel, pulls it out from his door and rubs off the sweat that has engulfed his body. He returns the towel to the door and spreads it out properly then nods delightfully. He stares at the statement that is boldly written on the front page of the notebook and reads it out to himself: "The face of the haunted". It does not please him anymore. He thought of his thoughts of a better title and 'Love also dies' storms his mind. He quickly draws two parallel lines across the former title. He does not know why he has to use that title but he has decided to use it. After all, a good title does not depict the story. He closes the book and places it beside the desk. He walks towards his hanger, picks up a shirt, dons it and walks towards the door. All of a sudden Mother Efuru and Mother Okwarama call him back in their usual chorus.

Chorus: It is danger outside.

Christopher: It's even dangerous staying inside. Anyway, let me take fresh air.

Chorus: The danger looms in the fresh air.

Christopher: But I'm becoming so uncomfortable sitting all alone in the room

Chorus: But we are here with you.

Christopher: Okay, I'll sit on the threshold.

Chorus: Go and dispose of that peel of drugs and then return for a newer work.

Christopher: I'll do that but what's your business with the drugs?

Chorus: Your well-being is also my duty.

Christopher: I'll do it but I need to take fresh air first. *(going out.)*

Chorus: A god is soon to be swallowed. *(Christpher opens the door, comes out, slams the door against himself and seats on the threshold.)* Tonight ends everything. *(Enter Boy (I) and Boy (II) in their usual wears, from the second door. They walk to the extreme and start waiting.)*

Boy (I): She say make I wait here

Boy (II): Say you sure say she go come?

Boy (I): She never give me fake appointment before.

Boy (II): Okay, make we wait and see *(EntersNgozi. Christopher catches a glimpse of her and is shocked. He rubs his palm over his face to see properly. Ngozi walks up to Boy (I). Boy (I) grabs her by her hand*

and pulls her to his side. She follows the pull so reluctantly and Boy (I) holds her wholly to himself. Christopher stands up and stares at them heartily.)

Boy (I): I think say you no go come.

Ngozi: Why would you think like that? Have I ever told you to wait for me before and I did not come?

Boy (I): No! But you know how girls behave - them no dey straightforward.

Ngozi: You said girls, but not Ngozi. *(They laugh.)*

Christopher:*(furiously)* Ngozi! *(Ngozi is shocked. She quickly releases herself from the grip of Boy (I). Christopher literarily disappears into the first door. Ngozi shivers in between the boys.)*

Boy (I): Ngozi, who be that? *(Ngozi ignores him.)* Who …? who …?   *(Christopher emerges from the second door.)*

Ngozi: Christopher, please, I am sorry.

Christopher: Ngozi. *(In-between tears)* What have I done to you? *(approaching her.)*

Ngozi: Please, I'm sorry. They … they … *(cannot find an excuse.)*

Christopher: You've … *(He pounces on her. He grabs her throat and they fall to the ground. Ngozi starts groaning. The boys rush at Christopher. They beat him and kick him. Boy(I) breaks a nearby bottle on his head and stabs him with it. They help Ngozi to her feet and she rushes at Christpher, feels his neck with the back of her palm, and lowers her ear to his heart to be sure he is still alive.)*

93

Boy (I): Leave am make we go!

Ngozi: You've killed him.

Boy (I): (*lowers his ear to his heart*) Make we commot here fast. (*Ngozi is reluctant to follow them but they drag her on and out of the platform. The stage light beams on Christopher on his pool of blood. He manages to get up and staggers out of the platform. He emerges from the first door with blood trailing behind him and staggers towards his door. He opens the door and staggers in. He staggers towards his desk and falls on the floor.*)

Christopher: (*gasps.*) Oh my God!

Chorus: Behold love dying with pregnancy. (*He stands up again and staggers towards the desk, runs his vibrating hand on the desk and pushes down the books. The notebook falls on the floor and the first page opens. He stops for a while and stares at it. The title – "Love also dies" now has meaning to him.*) But, it will be senseless.

Christopher: Senseless also is the mystery of this life.

Chorus: No! Christopher, No!

Christopher: There's no love on this earth. So of what use is living on? I've discovered that the love we profess towards our fellow men is not love but hatred at its highest vim.

Chorus: But you can still get the highest love in art.

Christopher: But art isn't complete without man. Love is also not complete without man. I know you do not understand merely because you're not man. Don't bother. I'm already satisfied with everything around me. I'm satisfied with art, I'm satisfied with man and I'm also satisfied with myself. (*falls from*

94

the stool—still losing blood.) Tonight unclasps my testament to the world. (*tears drip from his eyes and stream down his cheeks.*)

Chorus: It is all over. (*Christopher falls on the floor. Enter Ngozi, Johnson, Paul and Peter. Ngozi weeps. They rush into the door that is widely opened. They see Christopher lying on the floor. Johnson quickly rushes at him.*)

Johnson: Christopher! Christopher!

Christopher: Don't … bother. It … it … is … all over.

Johnson: No! It's not! Look at Ngozi here. (*Ngozi weeps.*)

Christopher: Tell my … people … my people … the … that the same … knowledge … I … I … have … come … to … acquire … have … have … ruined … m … me …

Johnson: No! Christopher, not yet! (*Christopher breathes his last and turns his face sideways*). Christopher! (*pauses. feels his neck, feels his hand. lowers his ear to his chest and shakes his head sorrowfully.*)

Peter: What's it?

Johnson: He is dead.

Ngozi: Dead? (*Paul stares beside him and finds the notebook. He picks it up and turns to the back page to know whether he has finished the work. He shakes his head and turns to Johnson.*)

Paul: I'll publish it for him. (*then to Ngozi.*) You've killed him so go ahead and enjoy yourself. (*walks out of the room and then out of the platform. Light beams on Christopher's body and then disappears.*)

95

THE END

THE FACE OF LOVE

Characters

Jude- a newly graduated student

Mama Jude his parents

Papa Jude

Chioma- his girl friend

Boy I

Boy II friends

Girl I

Girl II

Paul

Akin Cultists

Odinon

D.J.

Dancers

97

As light comes on the stage, we see a room. At the left hand side is the only entrance and exit door. The floor is covered with a carpet. Seats are seen at the corner of the wall, leaving only a narrow way to the door. The D.J. is busy arranging his musical instruments. Above the stage is an inscription: A Graduation Party. The room is already full with people. Enter Jude and his parents. Everybody stands up for them and starts clapping. Jude raises his hands and everywhere becomes silent again.

Jude: I welcome all of you to this party. I want you to feel free, drink and enjoy yourselves because this is the happiest day of my life. (*He turns towards the D.J. and signals to him to play his music. The D.J. screeches and everybody in the room praises him. All of a sudden he plays a mourning music and everybody becomes disappointed*).

Jude: D.J. what is the problem? Why not play a better music?

D.J: (*lowers the music*) I'm sorry! I really don't know what drove me into playing that music (*people still keep murmuring.*)

Boy I: (*To Girl I*) That music is only good for mourning. It can only be played in an atmosphere of death. This D.J. wants to spoil our mood.

Girl I: Forget it ! I thought he has apologized for his mistake (*Another music rends the room. And everybody begins to dance. Boy II left Girl II and walks up to Boy I. He calls him out from Girl I and they walk to a corner of the stage.*)

Boy II: James, there is something which I do not really understand.

Boy I: What is it?

Boy II: Is it because Jude graduated that his parents decided to stage this big party?

Boy I: Not really! So you have not heard? He graduated with a difference.

Boy II: How do you mean?

Boy I: He graduated with a first class.

Boy II: Are you sure it is not the kind of first class that is got through bribery?

Boy I: I don't know O. But I'm sure he merited it

Boy II: But I know him very well

Boy I: I know him well too.

Boy II: *(Lowers his voice)* Do you know he is a cultist-a member of the Black Axe Confraternity?

Boy I: I don't know this one. Who told you?

Boy II: His girlfriend, Chioma, told me.*(He pauses for a while and continues again.)* She said he joined the Black Axe Confraternity because of her.

Boy I: You don't mean it!

Boy II: He didn't want to lose her to any other boy.

Boy I: Though I don't know this, one thing I know is that Jude loves Chioma so much.

Boy II: Then how did he graduate with a first class?

Boy I: I don't know what to say. Well, intelligence is of nature and not of nurture.

Boy II: No, I disagree with you; nurture plays a very important role in the creation of great intelligence

Boy I: Then you are making reference to his home training.

Boy II: You have missed everything. It is through the parents that nature recreates and for that reason out of our parents we remain natural. Nurture on the other hand is of the society. The society makes us either good or bad; the society makes us intelligent or foolish.

Boy I: Emma, let's leave this talk for another time, Ogechi and Grace are coming *(Girl I and Girl II come close to them.)*

Girl I: James, what are you discussing with Emma? Come on, let's go and continue our dance, *(She drags Boy I out of that corner of the stage and they return to the dancing floor.)*

Girl II: Let's go back to the dancing floor.

Boy II: Grace, I don't feel like dancing.

Girl II: Then why did you bring me here? I hope it is not to watch others dance? *(She drags him.)* Common, let's go! *(Boy II follows her. Dance continues for a long time. And all of a sudden again, the D.J. makes the same mistake. He plays the mourning music. Everybody hisses. Jude, immediately emerges from the door, walks up to the D.J. and demands the CD plate. The D.J hands it over to him and he walks out through the door again. The D.J. puts another music and the dance continues. Enter ladies in beautiful robes, serving drinks. Enter* *again three boys dressed in black waers. Drinks are given to them. They refuse to dance. They rather walk straight to the seat and sit down. Enter Papa Jude. The music is lowered).*

Papa Jude: Ladies and gentlemen, I really don't know how to express my gratitude. But what I have to say is simple and it is that after this celebration we shall proceed to Mr. Fans for further celebration. *(Everybody claps for him.)* So keep enjoying yourselves. D.J, play more music – good music O! *(goes out of the platform. Dance continues. Boy I leaves Girl I to Boy II. Girl II tries to prevent Boy I from taking Boy II away, but Boy I promises the talk wouldn't take a long time. She allows Boy II go.)*

Boy I: I know you have come to call my attention to those three boys.

Boy I: So you have seen them too?

Boy II: When wolves come amidst Sheep their attributes reveal them to the world.

Boy II: They seem to have come to celebrate with their member.

Boy II: *(Carried away by their appearance)* I can see their faces: they are narrow like those of wild wolves. And their fingers sharpened like their claws, seeking for whom to devour. I sense blood…*(pauses)*Their looks depict that a pregnancy full of danger is about to be delivered.

Boy I: *(Beckons on him)* Have you started dreaming again?

Boy II: *(Turns to him.)*James, I'm not dreaming. Though dreams fulfil the reality…

Boy I: Please, let's talk about the reality, forget about dreams. (*One of the three boys stands up from among others and walks out of platform*) Emma, I think the danger you had earlier talked about is about to blast this little world of ours. I suggest we let our girls out of this pregnant world, until it is delivered of the hideous thing it is carrying.

Boy I: James, no! I say no! (*Every person in the dancing room overheard the scream and turn to see whose voice is overthrowing the blasting music*). Let them also witness the woe their fellows have brought upon the males world. (*Pauses.*) James, I have come to know that males merely claim to be brave; females are the true brave people. I have come to understand that bravery is not of strength, it is of the intellect. (*Girl II walks up to Boy II*).

Girl II: Emma, why have you come to embarrass yourself in this place? What…

Boy II: (*Cuts in*) Enough! Have you come to fault my intellect and posses my thought? Grace, go away for now. (*Grace walks out of the platform*).

Boy I: She has gone. Won't you stop her? Would you not let her witness the danger anymore? (*Enter one of the boys and Jude. They walk towards the others. The other two boys stand up and shake hands with Jude*).

Jude: You are welcome to my graduation party – Paul, Akin and Odinon.

Paul: We have come to bid you farewell, to the outside world. It is sad that you, of all people, is going out of our campus – our world.

Jude: Well, thank you for your concern. That is an experience that all of us who are one time undergraduates would for one day be faced with.

Boy II:(*Aside*) Wolves have plunged in to a trick, a coy, wiles and what will be the end result. The intellect will be dethroned and soiled.

Odinon: We want to go back to where we came from. Jude, we want you to pray for your departure.

Jude: I no longer understand this talk.

Akin: I am not interested in playing pun. We have come to avenge the death of Obi. The boy you killed in the examination hall.

Jude: (*terrified*) You mean Obi...O-bi please, please. (*Paul brings out a pistol and suddenly shoots to the roof of the building. Everybody freezes. The D.J. stops the music with immediate effect*).

Paul: Everybody on your knees! (*Everybody complies. Papa Jude rushes into the room*).

Papa Jude: What is it? What is it?

Paul: Your son murdered one of our members...

Papa Jude: Which member? I don't understand.

Paul: We are from the Viking Confraternity. He murdered one of us because his girlfriend loves the boy more than she loves him.

Papa Jude: Woe! This is not Jude. Jude can't do this. From whose breast has he sucked this evil? Woe!

Boy II: (*Cuts in*) Woe! Woe-men!

Odinon: (*turns back to see whose voice it is.*) Whose voice is it, whose woe wants to dethrone this earth? Ah, you? (*Points at Boy II*) Stand up! (*Boy II stands up and walks towards him.*) Explain what you have just said.

Boy II: What I mean is that the concept woman, or women, is got from two words woe and man or men.

Odinon: Bẹtter! (*Pauses*) Indeed, they have brought woe upon Jude.

Papa Jude: Please, leave him alone, don't kill him. Instead, let me give you any amount of money you want. Just don't!

Paul: Sorry sir, we don't think anything other than human life, can be equal to Obi's life.

Papa Jude: Okay then, take my life and leave his alone.

Paul: The joy of this campus tussle is to chop down the infant plantain at the expense of the mature one.

Papa Jude: Oh! Beast, oh! Man, oh! Earth, your heart is the *cruelest* of the entire universal creatures. (*Turns to Paul*) Look, sir, this boy whose life, whose soul would soon be snuffed out like that of a cock is my only son, my only soul, my only self…

Akin: Jude, say your last prayer or your last wish.

Jude: I wish to say the truth.

Akin: Okay, say it.

Jude: Everybody listen, I want everyone of you to learn from my own experience. I was a love fool; I was one of those who acted out of a sheer love for a girl and that love has given birth to this hatred. Please, do not count me among those who murdered for hatred's sake; count me among those who smothered a life that love may blossom and flower. *(Paul shoots him on the head and he falls to his face. Paul, Akin, and Odinon walk out of the stage. Papa Jude sits on the floor beside his dead son, weeping. Enter Mama Jude and Chioma).*

Papa Jude: Come and see this most piteous sight. Come and see how your son's blood weeps, preaching his innocence to the world. Just come and see how evil a woman could be. Come... *(Mama Jude weeps)*

THE END

THE

EARTHWORMS

Characters

Mr. Nzamzam

Mr Azubuike   Lecturers

Dr Okafore

Dr Dimpa

Onyekachi

Osinachi   Students

Tochukwu

Chinedu

Paul

Other Students

As light comes on stage, we see a Federal University hall with seats. Students have all settled down. Each of them is trying to make a quick revision. Enter Mr. Nzamzam, with heaps of exam scripts, followed by Mr. Azubuike. As they stand before the students, the class becomes quiet.

Mr. Nzamzam: (*keeps the heap of scripts on a nearby desk and quickly whispers something to Mr. Azubuike*) Everybody, remove ... your bags and your ... books! If I see ... any book on the table, (*He gnashes his teeth*) I will ... tear it into pieces. (*Students start removing their bags and their books. While some of the students hide papers containing some of the assumed answers under their tight-pants and stockings, Chinedu removes everything and remains calm*).

Mr. Azubuike: Today's exam is on Eng 601: Syntax and no more on Eng 608: History of English Language. (*Students begin to shout*)

Chinedu: (*quickly stands up*) But the schedule exam for today is History of English language and not Syntax!

Mr. Azubuike: *Sharrap* and sit down! (*Chinedu sits down.*) You are going to take it like that whether you like it or not. (*Students keep shouting*).

Chinedu: But sir, we did not prepare for that paper!

Azubuike:*Sharrap* I say, and sit down. (*Chinedusits down again. Azubuike turns and faces Mr. Nzamzam*) You can help me share the answer scripts. (*Mr. Nzamzam carries the scripts from the desk and starts sharing them within the students. The students collect the scripts amidst mumblings and grumblings. The students start filling the information that is required on the answer scripts*).

Mr. Nzamzam: You must face ... your work. If I catch you cough or laugh or shake or even move your neck ..., I will tear ... your paper.

Mr. Azubuike: This exam will last for only one hour thirty minutes. And as soon as I say submit, those who refused to submit immediately will have to take their scripts home for toilet. (*He starts sharing the question papers.*) If I give you the question paper, you start immediately. (*Students who are yet to get question papers start shouting: "But we have not got any!"*). That is your business. (*Students stand up and start struggling for the question papers while he is still holding them. He hisses and abandons the papers and they scatter on the floor. Students rush at the question papers and hurry back to their various seats. Mr. Azubuike returns to the front of the hall. Mr. Nzamzam walks up to him with a script in this hand*).

Mr. Nzamzam: (*Smiling*) I have caught ... one of them ... cheating.

Mr Azubuike: You caught one of them, you said?

Mr. Nzamzam: This is ... his script.

Mr. Azubuike: Why do you disturb yourself? Leave them, no matter what they write they can't pass. They would all fail the course.

Mr. Nzamzam: But one still needs ... to make the exam hall look ... tight.

Mr Azubuike: Oh you even have time to mark scripts. I don't mark at all

Mr.Nzamzam: How do you do it ... then?

Mr. Azubuike: You still ask questions. I hope you are not dashing these students marks? Marks are costly these days. You have to learn how to exchange good marks with good money and no money with missing scripts or better still carry-over.

Mr. Nzamzam: All that? I have already ... mastered them. Nobody passes my courses without ... oiling my palm.

Mr. Azubuike: Yes! Very good, that is one sure way you can buy a good car.

Mr. Nzamzam: But Mr. Azubuike, you have not told me ... how you manufacture your marks.

Mr. Azubuike: Marking these scripts is a waste of time. Anyway, I usually give it to one of them to mark, though with a very strict warning to make sure none, except himself, scores beyond forty per cent.

Mr Nzamzam: Ah! Mr. Azubuike, you don't know these students ... they would use it for their personal gain.

Mr Azubuike: I usually don't allow the same person record the scores.

Mr. Nzamzam: Ah, you are losing money o! (*Shrugs*) Well, that is your ... style. I wouldn't do so. (*Enter Dr. Okafore*). Here comes Dr. Okafore. What does he ... want here?

109

Dr. Okafore: Ah! Mr. Azubuike, I was just passing by er and I thought it important to see how your exam is going on.

Mr. Azubuike: What do they know and what can they write? (*Dr. Okafore seesa student cheating*).

Dr. Okafore: Look at that one (*points at the student*) Er you! What do you think you are doing er?

Mr. Azubuike: Dr. Okafore, why are you troubling yourself? Leave them to do whatever they like. They would all fail.

Dr. Okafore: Okay Mr Azubuike, I'm off to, er, Dr. Dimpa's office

Mr. Azubuike: Okay, please, greet Dr. Dimpa for me.

Dr. Okafore: Okay! (*Walks out of the hall*).

Mr. Nzamzam: Mr. Azubuike, are you not tired ... of waiting? Let's collect the papers.

Mr. Azubuike: I'm tired only that it isn't up to thirty minutes they started the exam.

Mr. Nzamzam: Does it matter?

Mr. Azubuike: You are right! After all they still would not pass. Stop them!

Mr. Nzamzam: Everybody stop... writing and submit your papers. (*Students startshouting disappointedly*). If you don't submit ... you would need to take it home. (*Some students quickly submit to Mr. Nzamzam. Mr. Nzamzam hands the submitted scripts to Mr. Azubuike and Mr. Azibuike leaves the hall with them. Suddenly there* *is a stampede. Students struggle to submit to Mr. Nzamzam who is also leaving. He waits, collects all the scripts and tearsthem. Students shout and start crying. Mr. Nzamzam leaves the hall while the students follow behind him).*

(Snooze)

In the same hall. Enter Chinedu, Osinachi, Tochukwu and Onyekachi.

Chinedu: I'm tired of this school; everything money, money, money. I'm not going to give any lecturer any unjustified money.

Tochukwu: You better do it; others have started to *sort* the courses, most especially Mr. Azubuike's and Mr. Nzamzam's courses.

Osinachi: I'll keep saying it till tomorrow, the only lecturer I respect in this University is Dr. Dimpa.

Onyekachi: What of Dr. Okafore?

Chinedu: That lecturer too is good. He is like Dr Dimpa. He doesn't collect money. But one thing is that you hardly can understand him.

Tochukwu: And I like him for it.

Chinedu: I like it too

111

Onyekachi: At least, that makes him unique. (*A student rushes into the hall*)

Osinachi: What's it, Paul?

Paul: You better go and *sort* Mr. Azubuike and Mr. Nzamzam's courses. They vowed to submit the results of all who refused to *sort* as missing scripts. (*Paul runs out of the hall. Osinachi stares into Chinedu's face, then at the others, shrugs and follows Paul immediately.*)

Tochukwu Let's go and *sort* those courses, else we will all fail.

Chinedu: I'll not sort it, besides I don't have money.

Tochukwu: I'm going. (*Tochukwu leaves. Onyekachi looks at Chinedu.*)

Onyekachi: Let's join them.

Chinedu: I won't go.

Onyekachi: Okay, bye! (*She also leaves*)

(Snooze)

Enter Chinedu, Tochukwu, Onyekachi, Paul and Osinachi.

Paul: Thank God, I scored two A's. One in Mr. Nzamzam's course and the other in Mr. Azubuike's course.

Tochukwu: What of in Dr. Dimpa and Dr. Okafore's courses?

Paul: I had Cs.

Tochukwu: I scored the same in Mr. Nzamzam's and Mr. Azubuike's courses, while I had a B in Dr. Dimpa's course and a C in Dr. Okafore's course.

Onyekachi: Chinedu, this one you are not celebrating with us what happened?

Osinachi: Leave him I told him to do what his mates were doing, but he refused now he has two missing scripts.

Paul: In which courses?

Osinachi: In Mr. Azubiuke's and Mr. Nzamzam's courses of course.

Chinedu: They are not even giving me attention.

Paul: This is what you would have avoided by just giving them money. That wouldn't stop you from being the intelligent boy you are.

Chinedu: No, I'll not pay for what I think I can write even when I'm woken from sleep. I'll meet them again. (*He leaves the hall.*)

THE END

THE PARASITE

Characters

Papa Oluchi   Husband

Mama paul

Mama Oluchi   Wives

New wife

Oluchi   Children

Paul

A room with two doors. A table occupies the centre of the stage and at its back is a bench. At the opposite side of the room is a cupboard with a transistor radio resting on it. The radio is heard blasting. And at the corner of the room is a hanger with all sort of clothes hanging on it.

Enter Mama Oluchi, with a plate of rice. She walks up to the table and places it on it. She turns her face towards the door, as if expecting somebody. She claps her hands.

Mama Oluchi: Oluchi! What is wrong with you this girl? Oluchi oo! This girl wants her father to kill me today as he almost did two days before yesterday. Oluchi!

Oluchi: (*answers from inside*)Yes mama!

Mama Oluchi: Are you deaf? Come on bring that cup of water.

Oluchi: (*enters with a cup of water.*) This is it ma. (*She places it on the table.*)

Mama Oluchi: Okay go and get me my kitchen stool. (*Exit Oluchi. Enter Mama Paul with a bowl of garri, and soup. She places it on the same table. And immediately Paul enters with a bowl of water. He places it on the floor under the table.*)

Mama Oluchi: Mama Paul, good morning! (*Exit Paul.*)

Mama Paul: I thought I have greeted you before.

Mama Oluchi: It still does not stop me from greeting you again.

Mama Paul: So you have already served your own plate of food.

Mama Oluchi: Yes oh, what would I do? I just pray that our husband accept to manage it because Oluchi couldn't go out to hawk the little mangoes I bought yesterday because she said she was not feeling fine.

Mama Paul: I am aware of it. How is she now?

Mama Oluchi: She said she is getting better. (*Enter Oluchi with a stool*) As I was saying it is from the leftover rice of yesterday I scooped this one I have brought for him. (*She collects the stool from her and sits on it*)

Mama Paul: Mama Oluchi, mine is also a left-over soup. Things are too hard these days that even when one brings one's goods out for sale, one hardly finds someone who will say 'how much?'

Mama Oluchi: That is how it is everywhere.

Mama Paul: And you know our husband hates being given leftover food.

Mama Oluchi: I have vowed I won't tell him that it is a leftover.

Mama Paul: Yours is better because he might not notice it. But you know he ate from the same soup yesterday.

Mama Oluchi: It is true o! (*pauses*) What are you going to do now?

Mama Paul: I can't do otherwise. After all since he married me into this house, he has never given me money to prepare food. Or has he given you?

Mama Oluchi: No! (*pauses*) But are you going to tell him so?

Mama Paul: In fact, I will summon courage this time and tell him— if he complains this time.

Mama Oluchi: ah! (*pauses*) My hands are not there. The last time that I couldn't bring him food in time he almost killed me with blows even when he gave me no money for the food. Do not think of telling him that he does not bring money.

Mama Paul: He will only beat me! He will beat me and that's all. Will I kill myself? (*Paul returns with a stool. She collects it and sits on it. Paul walks out again.*) Mama Oluchi, have you ever asked what he does with the salary they pay him at his workplace.

Mama Oluchi: I have been told that he uses them to chase young girls, girls as young as his own daughter, Oluchi.

Mama Paul: HIV infested girls. He would one day infest us with it. (*hears the footsteps of Papa Oluchi*) He is coming! (*They both adjust themselves. Papa Oluchi walks in from the other door. He is a middle-aged man with grey hair. He walks towards the bench. He stares into the faces of his two wives and sits down.*)

Papa Oluchi: (*clears his throat. He touches the plates of rice.*) Who brought this one?

Mama Oluchi: I did.

Papa Oluchi: (*frowns*) Why is the rice small and why is there only one piece of meat on it?

Mama Oluchi: There is ...

Papa Oluchi:*Sharp*! So you and your daughter have eaten the good part of the rice and only for you to bring this for me. (*pauses*) Well, I will eat it but emu ... emu ... (*starts eating. stops. opens the other bowl.*) Mama Paul, you brought this?

Mama Paul: Yes I did.

Papa Oluchi: (*opens the soup*) Che-yi! This same soup?

Mama Paul: Yes but let me explain?

Papa Oluchi: (*Stands up*) So you want to choke me with this soup ehn! (*Mama Paul tries to run away from his reach. He chases her and catches her. He beats her and she weeps and runs out of the stage.*) Just look at what she brought for me to eat! Just look at! (*pauses*) or would you say it is because of money. All the money you make every day who do you give them to? Or do you think I married you to be looking into your face. If you know you would not serve me with good food I send you back to your people. (*starts returning to the bench*) Stupid! (*sits down*) Where is the bowl of water so that I can wash my hands?

Mama Oluchi: Would you still eat the food?

Papa Oluchi: Ah ah, what do you mean? (*pauses*) So you want me to starve and die?

118

Mama Oluchi: That is not what I mean o.

Papa Oluchi: So you had better shut your useless mouth. (*He washes his hands and starts eating. After eating, he stands up and leaves the stage. Mama Oluchi clears the table*)

(snooze)

Enter Mama Oluchi and Mama Paul. They walk up to the bench and sit down.

Mama Oluchi: I hope you did not sustain any serious injury?

Mama Paul: Not really. Only that my back is aching. It seems it is going to swell and burst. I don't know how to treat it.

Mama Oluchi: Should I press it with hot water for you? Or are you going to take tablets?

Mama Paul: Please, press it with hot water for me. I will take tablets later.

Mama Oluchi: That is why I dread this husband of ours. He could kill with his hands. The last time he dealt with me he almost blindfolded me. If not for that chemist what is that his name?

Mama Paul: Emeka!

Mama Oluchi: Thank you! Emeka ... who gave me a medicine that I rubbed on the big ball that formed on my face.

119

By now, I would have become a blind woman. (*The footsteps of Papa Oluchi are heard.*) Our husband is coming. It seems with some other person. (*Enter Papa Oluchi with a young lady.*) Papa Oluchi, welcome o!

Mama Paul: Papa Oluchi welcome o!

Papa Oluchi: Thank you! (*pauses*) I had thought you would not greet me because my hands touched you. (*pauses*) Yes women, go and bring your stools. (*They both walk out and return with their little stools. They sit down while the lady is still standing.*) Sweety (*addressing the young lady. Smiles*) Come and sit down here. (*The young lady sits on the bench beside him. He smiles and clears his throat*) Mama Oluchi and Mama Paul, I want both of you to listen attentively. You see this lady, (*holding her*) the one you are seeing here, is now my last wife. (*pauses and frowns, looking into their faces.*) Do any of you have any objection?

Mama Oluchi & Mama Paul: No!

Papa Oluchi: Better (*stands up.*) I will be leaving you for now. I want both of you to tell her the tradition here. (*pauses*) I will return at night. (*points at both of them.*) Make sure my food becomes ready—three plates o! (*showing it with his fingers.*)

Mama Paul: Papa Oluchi, how is it going to be three?

Papa Oluchi: (*Surprised*) Mama Paul where did you get all this courage? (*pauses*) Let me just allow you today. (*pauses*) The three plates should include the new wife's own. (*He walks out of the platform.*)

Mama Oluchi: Mama Paul, how do we do the new wife's own ration?

120

New Wife: You people should not worry about me I have eaten.

Mama Paul: It seems you do not understand.

New Wife: Understand what?

Mama Paul: That you are expected to present your own plate of food to him when he comes back at night.

New wife: I still don't understand. But he gave no money for the food.

Mama Oluchi: Who talks about money for food in this house?

New Wife: And how do you cook? How do you feed?

Mama Paul: We borrow capital, buy fruits like mangoes and hawk or sell by the roadside ...

New Wife: And after which you serve him food?

Mama Paul: Yes o, my daughter!

New Wife: But he works!

Mama Oluchi: Yes, but we don't see the money.

New Wife: No! (*pauses*) The time has come when women have to stand for their rights. The time has come when the responsibilities of a man and a woman are clearly defined. The time has come when women will no longer be seen as second-class citizens: we are co-owners of this earth.

Mama Paul: Yes, I support you, my daughter.

Mama Oluchi: ah! (*pauses*) My hands are not there. If Papa Oluchi notices this talk ... ah ...

Mama Paul: Mama Oluchi, what our co-wife is talking is the truth. Our husband ought to take care of us, feed us and our children and not the other way round.

New Wife: We shall from this moment fight for our rights and the rights of women universally. (*They walk out of the stage.*)

(Snooze)

Enter Mama Oluchi with a plate well covered. Enter Mama Paul with another plate covered. Enter Papa Oluchi. Papa Oluchi walks to the bench and sits down. Enter New Wife, with a plate covered. They place them on the table.

Papa Oluchi: Sweety. Let me first of all taste your own food. Let me know if you know how to cook. (*He opens the plate.*) Sweety! What is this? An empty plate!

New Wife: (*stands, frowns, hands akimbo.*) What you saw inside the plate was what you gave.

Papa Oluchi: So Mama Oluchi and Mama Paul didn't tell you the tradition here. (*pauses*) Okay! It is just because you are new. (*opens that of Mama Oluchi*) What! An empty plate also! (*pauses. stares at them all and opens that of Mama Paul quickly*) What is all these?

New Wife: You gave nothing, you will receive nothing.

122

Papa Oluchi: I know you are the cause of all these. Look, I had merely wanted to help solve your marriage problem because I thought you are hard working only for you to turn my other wives against me. (*Enraged*) *Oya* go, I am no longer interested in the marriage.

Mama Paul: No! She is going nowhere! She is now part of this house.

Papa Oluchi: Grace, please go. I am not marrying you again.

Mama Oluchi: Oh! Is it because she told the truth? (*pauses*) So you have been cheating us since all these days.

Papa Oluchi: Mama Oluchi, common *sharp* and go and get me something to eat!

Mama Oluchi: Listen, Papa Oluchi, as from this moment you will not taste my food unless you bring money for food.

Papa Oluchi: *Chineke e*! (*Surprised*) You, Mama Paul ...

Mama Paul: If you call my name there *Amadioha* will strike your mouth.

Papa Oluchi: Okay, Grace please beg them to give me a little food to eat. Just a little so that I will not go to bed in an empty stomach. And in subsequent times I will always give money for food.

New wife: No! (*pauses*) You must sleep in an empty stomach tonight. So that those girls you give your money ... in fact, wives, let's leave him. (*They walk out of the stage.*)

THE END

Owerri—Ibadan—Port Harcourt—Iyamho

2004—2016

Mmap Fiction Series

If you have enjoyed *The Policeman Also Dies and Other Plays* consider these other fine books in **Mmap Fiction Series** from *Mwanaka Media and Publishing*:

The Water Cycle by Andrew Nyongesa
A Conversation…, A Contact by Tendai Rinos Mwanaka
A Dark Energy by Tendai Rinos Mwanaka
Keys in the River: New and Collected Stories by Tendai Rinos Mwanaka
How The Twins Grew Up/Makurire Akaita Mapatya by Milutin Djurickovic and Tendai Rinos Mwanaka
White Man Walking by John Eppel
The Big Noise and Other Noises by Christopher Kudyahakudadirwe
Tiny Human Protection Agency by Megan Landman
Ashes by Ken Weene and Umar O. Abdul
Notes From A Modern Chimurenga: Collected Struggle Stories by Tendai Rinos Mwanaka
Another Chance by Chinweike Ofodile
Pano Chalo/Frawn of the Great by Stephen Mpashi, translated by Austin Kaluba
Kumafulatsi by Wonder Guchu

Soon to be released

School of Love and Other Stories by Ricardo Felix Rodriguez

https://facebook.com/MwanakaMediaAndPublishing/

Printed in the United States
by Baker & Taylor Publisher Services